IT'S A NEW DAY
FOR FINANCIAL FREEDOM

BIBLICAL FINANCIAL STUDY

LIFE GROUP MANUAL

D1636860

Crown Financial Ministries™

CROWN.ORG

MY LIFE GROUP

Day and time it meets: _____   Date of first meeting: _____

Where it meets: _____

My leaders: _____   Phone: _____

_____   Phone: _____

Note: Any regularly scheduled meeting that falls on a holiday or other special event may be rescheduled.

ISBN 13: 978-1-56427-237-9

Verses identified as (AMPLIFIED) are taken from the *Amplified® Bible*, © 1954, 1958, 1962, 1964, 1965, 1987 by The Lockman Foundation. Used by permission.

Verses identified as (KJV) are taken from the *King James Version*.

Verses identified as (NIV) are taken from the *Holy Bible: New International Version*, © 1973, 1978, 1984 by the International Bible Society. Used by permission of Zondervan Bible Publishers.

Verses identified as (TLB) are taken from *The Living Bible*, © 1971 by Tyndale House Publishers, Wheaton, Illinois. Used by permission.

All other Scripture quotations are taken from the *New American Standard Bible®* (Updated Edition) (NASB), © 1960, 1962, 1963, 1968, 1971, 1972, 1973, 1975, 1977, 1995 by The Lockman Foundation. Used by permission.

July 2008 Edition

LIFE GROUP SCHEDULE

WELCOME!

We are so thankful that you have decided to participate in Crown's *Biblical Financial Study*. God has used the principles you are about to learn in the lives of hundreds of thousands of people who have taken this life group study. We've learned that people benefit most when they are faithful to complete the following.

First of all, before your life group meets, read *Your Money Counts*. This book is easy to read and will provide you with a good overview of the study. Then, complete these requirements before each weekly meeting.

1. Homework

Complete the homework in writing. The homework questions are designed to take only about 15 minutes each day to complete. Space is provided in the *Life Group Manual* to answer the questions. If a married couple takes the study together, each will use a separate *Life Group Manual*.

2. Scripture Memory

Memorize an assigned passage from the Bible each week and individually recite the verse(s) at the beginning of the meeting. This will help you remember the most important principles.

3. Practical Application

Complete a practical financial exercise, such as beginning a spending plan or designing a debt repayment plan.

4. Prayer

Everyone prays for the other group members each day. Answers to prayers are one of the most encouraging parts of the life group experience.

> If someone is unable to complete the requirements for a particular week, we've asked the leaders not to have him or her participate in that meeting's discussion. This accountability helps us to be faithful. And the more faithful we are, the more benefits we receive from the study.

Attendance. Everyone should attend at least eight of the 10 weekly meetings. Please notify one of the leaders in advance if you anticipate missing a meeting or arriving late. The meetings are designed to begin and end on time.

Again, we are very grateful for your participation in the *Biblical Financial Study*. I pray that the Lord will bless you in every way as you learn His financial principles.

Howard Dayton

Howard Dayton, Author
Cofounder, Crown Financial Ministries

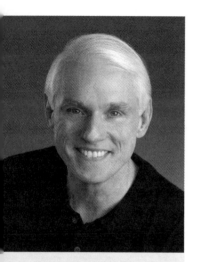

**HOWARD DAYTON,
CROWN COFOUNDER**

PURPOSE

***The purpose of the** Biblical Financial Study* ***
is to teach people God's financial principles
in order to know Christ more intimately
and to be free to serve Him.***

FINANCIAL POLICY

- Crown Financial Ministries does not endorse, recommend, or sell any financial investments. No one may use affiliation with Crown to promote or influence the sale of any financial products or services.

- Crown's *Biblical Financial Study* does not give specific investment advice. No one may use his or her affiliation with Crown to give investment advice.

- Kingdom Advisors, led by Ron Blue and founded by Larry Burkett, is devoted to equipping Christian financial advisors to apply biblical wisdom to their advice and counsel. To learn more about the organization and its Qualified Kingdom Advisor™ designation, please visit KingdomAdvisors.org.

- This study is affordably priced because we do not want cost to be an obstacle to people who desire to participate. If you find the study valuable and want to help make it available to others, you may make a tax-deductible gift to Crown Financial Ministries.

WEB SITE

Crown has designed a Web site as a resource to provide life group members and leaders with up-to-date and detailed financial information. It contains helpful articles, a categorized list of the verses dealing with possessions, links to other useful Web sites, and much more.

Visit the Web site at Crown.org for a world of information.

PERSONAL INFORMATION

A critical ingredient of taking part in a life group study is what happens *after* the study. It is our desire to provide important and useful resources and information that will assist you as you walk in the principles you are learning in this study. For us to do this we need to know who you are and how to get this information to you.

Please take a moment right now and complete the Life Group Enrollment Form online in the "My Crown" section of Crown.org. When you enroll as a life group member, you will have access to helpful tools and information to assist you during this study.

"Therefore if you have not been faithful in the use of worldly wealth, who will entrust the true riches to you?" (Luke 16:11).

INTRODUCTION

WEEK 1

How we handle money impacts our relationship with the Lord.

PRE-MEETING WORK

INTRO

Scripture to Memorize

"Therefore if you have not been faithful in the use of worldly* wealth, who will entrust the true riches to you?" (Luke 16:11).

* The word *worldly* from the New International Version has been substituted for the word *unrighteous* from the *New American Standard Bible* to clarify the meaning of this passage.

Practical Application

In addition to memorizing the Scripture above and completing the Homework below, read *Your Money Counts* prior to the first meeting. Please fill out your Life Group Member Enrollment Form online at Crown.org. In the *Crown Money Map,*™ review the definition of "True Financial Freedom" and complete the "My Life Purpose" section.

Homework

1. What was the most helpful information you learned from reading *Your Money Counts*?

Read Isaiah 55:8-9.

2. Based on this passage, do you think God's financial principles will differ from how most people handle money? What do you think would be the greatest difference?

Read Luke 16:11.

3. What does this verse communicate to you about the importance of managing possessions faithfully?

4. How does handling money impact our fellowship with the Lord?

Scripture memory helps

The memory verses cards are found in the back of the _Practical Application Workbook_ and are designed to be removed and carried with you throughout the day.

TO BE READ BEFORE COMPLETING YOUR WEEK 2 HOMEWORK

This study will transform your life and finances as you learn what the God of the universe says about handling money. And the study is for everyone—single or married, young or old, whether you earn a lot or a little.

The way most people handle money is in sharp contrast to God's financial principles. Isaiah 55:8 says it this way, *"'For my thoughts are not your thoughts, neither are your ways my ways,' declares the Lord"* (NIV). The most significant difference between the two is that the Bible reveals God is closely involved with our finances. Many people fail to realize it because He has chosen to be invisible to us and to operate in the unseen supernatural realm.

THE BIBLE AND MONEY

It may surprise you to learn how much the Bible says about finances. More than 2,350 verses address God's way of handling money and possessions. Jesus Christ said more about money than almost any other subject, and He did it for three reasons.

1. How we handle money impacts our fellowship with God.

Jesus equates how we handle our money with the quality of our spiritual life. In Luke 16:11, He says, *"Therefore if you have not been faithful in the use of worldly* wealth, who will entrust the true riches to you?"* The true riches in life are a close relationship with the Lord.

If we handle money according to the principles of Scripture, we enjoy closer fellowship with Christ. The parable of the talents demonstrates this as the master congratulates the servant who managed his money faithfully: *"Well done, good and faithful [servant]. You were faithful with a few things, I will put you in charge of many things; enter into the joy of your master"* (Matthew 25:21). We can enter into the joy of a more intimate relationship with God as we handle money His way.

MONEY IS A PRIMARY COMPETITOR WITH CHRIST FOR OUR AFFECTION.

2. Money and possessions compete with the Lord for first place in our lives.

Money is a primary competitor with Christ for our affection. Jesus tells us we must choose to serve only one of these two masters. *"No one can serve two masters. Either he will hate the one and love the other, or he will be devoted to the one and despise the other. You cannot serve both God and money"* (Matthew 6:24, NIV). We use money, but it is impossible for us to serve money and still serve and love God.

During the Crusades of the 12th Century, the Crusaders hired mercenaries to fight for them. Because it was a religious war, the mercenaries were baptized before fighting. Before going under the water, the soldiers would take their swords and hold them up out of the water to symbolize that Jesus Christ was not in control of their weapons. They claimed freedom to use their weapons in any way they wished.

Unfortunately, that illustrates the way many people today handle their money as they hold their wallet or purse "out of the water." Their attitude is, "God, you may be Lord of my entire life except in the area of money—I am perfectly capable of handling that myself."

3. God wants us to be money smart.

The Lord also talked so much about money because He knew that money problems would be a challenge for all of us. Because He loves and cares for us so deeply, He wanted to equip us to make the wisest possible financial decisions.

A DIVISION OF RESPONSIBILITIES

Years ago, a close friend, Jim Seneff, asked me to join him in a study of the Bible to discover what God said about money. We carefully read through it, identifying each of the 2,350 verses related to money and possessions and arranging them by topic. Not only were we surprised by how practical they were, we discovered an important pattern: a division of responsibilities in the handling of money. Simply put, God has a role, and we have a role. You may also be surprised as you learn in this study which responsibilities are God's and which are yours.

THE CROWN MONEY MAP

We have developed the *Crown Money Map*™ to help you begin your journey to true financial freedom. The Money Map will enable you to identify where you are, where you want to be and your next step to take for financial progress. A full-color copy of the map has been provided in the *Practical Application Workbook*.

THREE FEATURES

This study includes three features to assist you on your journey to true financial freedom.

CrownMoneyMap.org. CrownMoneyMap.org is a dynamic Web site created to accompany this study. It contains online tools, videos, and answers to frequently asked questions. You can personalize your journey to true financial freedom, track your progress, and store and modify information—even share it with others in the Money Map community! Join us and be encouraged.

Roadside Assistance—Online! At the end of most lessons in the *Practical Application Workbook*, *Roadside Assistance—Online!* identifies free online tools, forms, information, and assistance you can access in the "My Crown" section of Crown.org.

Tools for the Journey. At the end of applicable lessons in the *Practical Application Workbook*, we recommend outstanding books, Web sites, financial tools, and organizations that will help you on your journey.

As I wrote this study, I often prayed that you would experience the tremendous sense of hope, peace and confidence that comes from discovering God's way of handling money. I am excited because I know that great things are in store for you.

MY NOTES

"Everything in the heavens and earth is yours, O Lord"
(1 Chronicles 29:11, TLB).

GOD'S PART & OUR PART

WEEK 2

The Lord is
Owner of all.

HOMEWORK

Scripture to Memorize

"Everything in the heavens and earth is yours, O Lord, and this is your kingdom. We adore you as being in control of everything. Riches and honor come from you alone, and you are the Ruler of all mankind; your hand controls power and might and it is at your discretion that men are made great and given strength" (1 Chronicles 29:11-12, TLB).

Practical Application

Complete the Personal Financial Statement, begin keeping a record of everything you spend, and complete the Quit Claim Deed (bring it to class to be witnessed by members of your group). Find your location on the *Crown Money Map*™ and also review Destination 1.

Day One - Let's Review the Introduction

Read the Introduction Notes on pages 10-11 and answer:

1. What information especially interested you?

2. Comment on any personal challenges you felt after learning the three reasons the Bible says so much about money.

GOD'S PART AND OUR PART

Day Two

Read Deuteronomy 10:14; Psalm 24:1; and 1 Corinthians 10:26.

1. What do these passages teach about the ownership of your possessions?

Read Leviticus 25:23; Psalm 50:10-12; and Haggai 2:8.

2. What are some of the specific items that God owns?

Leviticus 25:23 -

Psalm 50:10-12 -

Haggai 2:8 -

3. Prayerfully evaluate your attitude of ownership toward your possessions. Do you consistently recognize the true owner of those possessions? Give two practical suggestions to help recognize God's ownership.

Day Three

Read 1 Chronicles 29:11-12 and Psalm 135:6.

1. What do these verses say about God's control of circumstances?

Read Proverbs 21:1; Isaiah 40:21-24; and Acts 17:26.

2. What do these passages tell you about God's control of people?

Proverbs 21:1 -

Isaiah 40:21-24 -

Acts 17:26 -

3. Do you normally recognize the Lord's control of all events? If not, how can you become more consistent in recognizing His control?

Day Four

Read Genesis 45:4-8; Genesis 50:19-20; and Romans 8:28.

1. Why is it important to realize that God controls and uses even difficult circumstances for good in the life of a godly person?

2. How does this perspective impact you today?

3. Share a difficult circumstance you have experienced and how God ultimately used it for good in your life.

Day Five

Read Psalm 34:9-10; Matthew 6:31-33; and Philippians 4:19.

1. What has the Lord promised concerning meeting your needs?

2. Give an example from the Bible of the Lord providing for someone's needs in a supernatural way.

3. How does this apply to you today?

Day Six

Read 1 Corinthians 4:2.

1. According to this verse what is your requirement as a steward?

2. How would you define a steward?

Read Luke 16:1-2.

3. Why did the master remove the steward from his position?

Read Luke 16:10.

4. Describe the principle found in this verse.

5. How does this apply in your situation?

Follow-up

☑ Please write your prayer requests in your prayer log before coming to the meeting.

☑ I will take the following action as a result of this week's study:

This is the most important section of the entire study, because how we view God determines how we live. In the Bible God calls Himself by more than 250 names. The name that best describes God's part in the area of money is Lord.

After losing his children and all his possessions, Job continued to worship God because he knew His role as Lord of those possessions. Moses walked away from the treasures of Egypt, choosing instead to suffer with God's people because he accepted God's role as Lord of all. There are three parts to God's position as Lord.

GOD'S PART

OWNERSHIP

God owns all our possessions. *"To the Lord your God belong . . . the earth and everything in it"* (Deuteronomy 10:14, NIV). *"The earth is the Lord's, and all it contains"* (Psalm 24:1).

Scripture even reveals specific items God owns. Leviticus 25:23 identifies Him as the owner of all the land: *"The land . . . shall not be sold permanently, for the land is Mine."* Haggai 2:8 says that He owns the precious metals: *"'The silver is Mine and the gold is Mine,' declares the Lord of hosts."* And in Psalm 50 we are told that God owns the animals.

> *"Every beast of the forest is Mine, the cattle on a thousand hills . . . everything that moves in the field is Mine. If I were hungry, I would not tell you, for the world is Mine, and all it contains"* (Psalm 50:10-12).

God created all things, and He never transferred the ownership of His creation to people. In Colossians 1:17 we are told that, *"In Him all things hold together."* At this very moment the Lord holds everything together by His power. As we will see throughout this study, recognizing God's ownership is crucial in allowing Jesus Christ to become the Lord of our money and possessions.

BY STUDYING THE BIBLE WE CAN EXPAND OUR VISION OF WHO GOD IS.

Our Ownership or His Lordship?

If we are to be genuine followers of Christ, we must transfer ownership of our possessions to Him. *"None of you can be My disciple who does not give up all his own possessions"* (Luke 14:33). Sometimes He tests us by asking us to give up the very possessions that are most important to us.

The most vivid example of this in the Bible is when God instructed Abraham, *"Take now your son, your only son, whom you love, Isaac . . . and offer him there as a burnt offering"* (Genesis 22:2). When Abraham obeyed, demonstrating his willingness to give up his most valuable possession, God responded, *"Do not lay a hand on the boy . . . now I know that you fear God, because you have not withheld from Me your son"* (Genesis 22:12, NIV).

When we acknowledge God's ownership, every spending decision becomes a spiritual decision. No longer do we ask, "Lord, what do You want me to do with my money?" It becomes, "Lord, what do You want me to do with Your money?" When we have this attitude and handle His money according to His wishes, spending and saving decisions become as spiritual as giving decisions.

God's ownership also influences how we care for possessions. For example, because the Lord is the owner of where we live we want to please Him by keeping His home or apartment cleaner and in better repair!

Recognizing God's Ownership

Our culture—the media, even the law—says that what you possess, you own. Acknowledging God's ownership requires a transformation of thinking, and this can be difficult. It is easy to believe intellectually that God owns all you have but still live as if this were not true.

Here are several practical suggestions to help us recognize God's ownership.

- For the next 30 days, meditate on 1 Chronicles 29:11-12 when you first awake and just before going to sleep.
- Be careful in the use of personal pronouns; consider substituting "the" or "the Lord's" for "my," "mine," and "ours."
- For the next 30 days, ask God to make you aware of His ownership.
- Establish the habit of acknowledging God's ownership every time you purchase an item.

Recognizing God's ownership is important in learning contentment. When you believe you own a particular possession, circumstances surrounding it will affect your attitude. If it's favorable, you will be happy, if it's a difficult circumstance, you will be discontent.

Shortly after Jim came to grips with God's ownership, he purchased a car. He had driven the car only two days before someone rammed into the side of it. Jim's first reaction was "Lord, I don't know why You want a dent in Your car, but now You've got a big one!" Jim was learning contentment!

CONTROL

Besides being Creator and Owner, God is ultimately in control of every event. *"We adore you as being in control of everything"* (1 Chronicles 29:11, TLB). *"Whatever the Lord pleases, He does, in heaven and in earth"* (Psalm 135:6). And in the book of Daniel, King Nebuchadnezzar stated: *"I praised the Most High; I honored and glorified Him who lives forever. . . . He does as He pleases with the powers of heaven and the peoples of the earth. No one can hold back His hand or say to him: 'What have you done?'"* (Daniel 4:34-35, NIV).

God is also in control of difficult events. *"I am the Lord, and there is no other, the One forming light and creating darkness, causing well-being and creating calamity; I am the Lord who does all these"* (Isaiah 45:6-7).

It is important for us to realize that our heavenly Father uses even seemingly devastating circumstances for ultimate good in the lives of the godly. *"We know that God causes all things to work together for good to those who love God, to those who are*

GOD IS ULTIMATELY IN CONTROL OF EVERY EVENT.

called according to His purpose" (Romans 8:28). The Lord allows difficult circumstances for three reasons.

1. He accomplishes His intentions.

This is illustrated in the life of Joseph, who was sold into slavery as a teenager by his jealous brothers. Joseph later said to his brothers: *"Do not be distressed and do not be angry with yourselves for selling me here, because it was to save lives that God sent me ahead of you. . . . It was not you who sent me here, but God. . . . You intended to harm me, but God intended it for good"* (Genesis 45:5, 8; 50:20, NIV).

2. He develops our character.

Godly character, something that is precious in the sight of God, is often developed during trying times. *"We also rejoice in our sufferings, because we know that suffering produces perseverance; perseverance, character"* (Romans 5:3-4, NIV).

3. He disciplines His children.

> *"Those whom the Lord loves He disciplines. . . . He disciplines us for our good, so that we may share His holiness. All discipline for the moment seems not to be joyful, but sorrowful; yet to those who have been trained by it, afterwards it yields the peaceful fruit of righteousness"* (Hebrews 12:6, 10-11).

When we are disobedient, we can expect our loving Lord to discipline us, often through difficult circumstances. His purpose is to encourage us to abandon our sin and "share His holiness." You can be at peace knowing that your loving heavenly Father is in control of every situation you will ever face. He will use every one of them for a good purpose.

REGARDLESS OF HOW HE CHOOSES TO PROVIDE FOR OUR NEEDS, GOD IS COMPLETELY RELIABLE.

GOD IS THE PROVIDER

The Lord promises to provide our needs. *"Seek first His kingdom and His righteousness, and all these things [food and clothing] shall be given to you"* (Matthew 6:33, NIV).

The same Lord who fed manna to the children of Israel during their 40 years of wandering in the wilderness and who fed 5,000 with only five loaves and two fish has promised to provide our needs. This is the same Lord who told Elijah, *"I have commanded the ravens to provide for you. . . . The ravens brought him bread and meat in the morning and bread and meat in the evening"* (1 Kings 17:4, 6).

God is both predictable and unpredictable. God is totally predictable in His faithfulness to provide for our needs. What we cannot predict is how He will provide. He uses different and often surprising means—an increase in income or a gift. He may provide an opportunity to stretch limited resources through money-saving purchases. Regardless of how He chooses to provide for our needs, God is completely reliable.

Charles Allen tells a story that illustrates this principle. As World War II was drawing to a close, the Allied armies gathered up many orphans and placed them in camps where they were well fed. But despite excellent care, the orphans were afraid and slept poorly.

Finally, a doctor came up with a solution. When the children were put to bed, he gave each of them a piece of bread to hold. Any hungry children could get more to eat, but when they were finished, they would still have this piece of bread just to hold—not to eat.

This piece of bread produced wonderful results. The children went to bed knowing instinctively they would have food to eat the next day. That guarantee gave them restful sleep.

Similarly, God has given us His guarantee—our "piece of bread." As we cling to His promises of provision, we can relax and be content. *"My God shall supply all your needs according to His riches . . ."* (Philippians 4:19).

Needs Versus Wants

The Lord instructs us to be content when our basic needs are met. *"If we have food and clothing, we will be content"* (1 Timothy 6:8, NIV). It is important to understand the difference between a need and a want. Needs are the basic necessities of life—food, clothing, and shelter. Wants are anything in excess of needs. God may allow us to have our wants, but He has not promised to provide all of them.

GETTING TO KNOW GOD

God, as He is revealed in Scripture, is much different than most people imagine. We tend to shrink Him down to our human abilities and limitations, forgetting that He *"stretched out the heavens and laid the foundations of the earth"* (Isaiah 51:13). By studying the Bible we can expand our vision of who He is. The following are a just a few samples.

He is Lord of the universe.

Carefully review some of His names and attributes: Creator, the Almighty, eternal, all-knowing, all-powerful, awesome, Lord of lords, and King of kings. God's power and ability are beyond our understanding.

Astronomers estimate that there are more than 100 billion galaxies in the universe, each containing billions of stars. The distance from one end of a galaxy to the other is often measured in millions of light years. Though our sun is a relatively small star, it could contain more than one million earths, and it has temperatures of 20 million degrees at its center. Isaiah wrote, *"Lift up your eyes on high and see who has created these stars. . . . He calls them all by name; because of the greatness of His might and the strength of His power, not one of them is missing"* (Isaiah 40:26).

He is Lord of the nations.

God established the nations. Acts 17:26 says, *"He [the Lord] . . . scattered the nations across the face of the earth. He decided beforehand which should rise and fall, and when. He determined their boundaries"* (TLB).

God is far above all national leaders and powers. Isaiah 40:21-23 tells us, *"Do you not know? Have you not heard? . . . It is He who sits above the circle of the earth, and its inhabitants are like grasshoppers. . . . He it is who reduces rulers to nothing, who makes the judges of the earth meaningless."* From Isaiah 40:15, 17 we read, *"The nations are like a drop from a bucket, and are regarded as a speck of dust on the scales. . . . All the nations are as nothing before Him."*

HeyHoward@Crown.org

Q: *I'm totally frustrated! God says He's going to provide my needs. So, what's there for me to do? Do I have to go to work?*

A: God has certain responsibilities when it comes to money, and He's given others to us. He's promised to provide our needs, and at the same time He wants us to work hard—for many reasons. He usually provides our needs through our work.

GOD IS MUCH DIFFERENT THAN MOST PEOPLE IMAGINE.

He is Lord of the individual.

Psalm 139:3-4, 16 reveals God's involvement with each of us as individuals. *"You are familiar with all my ways. Before a word is on my tongue you know it completely, O Lord. . . . All the days ordained for me were written in your book before one of them came to be"* (NIV). The Lord is so involved in our lives that He reassures us, *"The very hairs of your head are all numbered"* (Matthew 10:30). Our heavenly Father is the One who knows us the best and loves us the most.

God hung the stars in space, fashioned the earth's towering mountains and mighty oceans, and determined the destiny of nations. Jeremiah observed: *"Nothing is too difficult for You"* (Jeremiah 32:17). Yet God knows when a sparrow falls to the ground. Nothing in this study is more important than catching the vision of who God is and what responsibilities He retains in our finances.

SUMMARY OF GOD'S PART

The Lord did not design people to shoulder the responsibilities that only He can carry. Jesus said, *"Come to Me, all who are weary and heavy-laden, and I will give you rest. Take My yoke upon you. . . . For My yoke is easy, and My burden is light"* (Matthew 11:28-30). God has assumed the burdens of ownership, control, and provision. For this reason, His yoke is easy and we can rest and enjoy the peace of God.

For most of us, the primary problem is failing to consistently recognize God's part. Our culture believes that God plays no part in financial matters, and we have, in some measure, been influenced by that view.

Another reason for this difficulty is that God has chosen to be invisible. Anything that is "out of sight" tends to become "out of mind." We get out of the habit of recognizing His ownership, control, and provision.

After learning God's part, you might wonder whether He's left any responsibilities for us. The Lord has given us great responsibility.

OUR PART

The word that best describes our part is *steward*. A steward is a manager of someone else's possessions. God has given us the authority to be stewards. *"You made him ruler over the works of your [the Lord's] hands; you put everything under his feet"* (Psalm 8:6, NIV).

A STEWARD IS A MANAGER OF SOMEONE ELSE'S POSSESSIONS.

Our responsibility is summed up in this verse: *"It is required of stewards that one be found faithful"* (1 Corinthians 4:2). Before we can be faithful, we must know what we are required to do. Just as the purchaser of a complicated piece of machinery studies the manufacturer's manual to learn how to operate it, we need to examine the Creator's handbook—the Bible—to determine how He wants us to handle His possessions.

As we begin to study our responsibilities, it's important to remember that God loves and cares for us deeply. He is a God of mercy and grace. He has given us these principles because He wants the best for us. Most people discover areas in which they have not been faithful. Don't become discouraged. Simply seek to apply faithfully what you learn.

Now, let's examine two important elements of our responsibility.

1. Be faithful with what we are given.

We are to be faithful regardless of how much God entrusts to us. The parable of the talents (a talent was a sum of money) illustrates this. *"It will be like a man going on a journey, who called his servants and entrusted his property to them. To one he gave five talents of money, to another two talents, and to another one talent"* (Matthew 25:14-15, NIV).

When the owner returned, he held each one responsible for faithfully managing his possessions. The owner praised the faithful servant who received five talents: *"Well done, good and faithful [servant]. You were faithful with a few things, I will put you in charge of many things; enter into the joy of your master"* (Matthew 25:21). Interestingly, the servant who had been given two talents received the identical reward as the one who had been given five (see Matthew 25:23). God rewards faithfulness regardless of the amount over which we are responsible.

We are required to be faithful whether we are given much or little. As someone once said, "It's not what I would do if $1 million were my lot; it's what I am doing with the $10 I've got."

2. Be faithful in every area.

God wants us to be faithful in handling all of our money. Unfortunately, most Christians have been taught how to handle only 10 percent of their income God's way—the area of giving. And although this area is crucial, so is the other 90 percent, which they frequently handle from the world's perspective.

Study this diagram. As a result of not being taught to handle money biblically, many Christians have wrong attitudes toward possessions. This often causes them to make poor financial decisions with painful consequences. Hosea 4:6 reads, *"My people are destroyed for lack of knowledge."*

BENEFITS OF HANDLING MONEY FAITHFULLY

The faithful steward enjoys three benefits.

1. More Intimate Fellowship with Jesus Christ

Remember what the master said to the servant who had been faithful with his finances: *"Enter into the joy of your master"* (Matthew 25:21). We can enter into closer fellowship with our Lord when we are faithful with the possessions He has given us.

Someone once told me that God often allows a person to teach a subject because the teacher desperately needs it! That is true for me in the area of money. I have never met anyone who had more wrong attitudes about money or who handled money more contrary to Scripture than I did. When I began to apply these principles, I experienced a dramatic improvement in my fellowship with the Lord—exactly what He intended.

2. The Development of Character

God uses money to refine character. As David McConaugh explained in his book, *Money the Acid Test* (written in 1918), "Money, most common of temporal things, involves uncommon and eternal consequences. Even though it may be done quite unconsciously, money molds people in the process of getting it, saving it, spending it, and giving it. Depending on how it's used, it proves to be a blessing or a curse. Either the person becomes master of the money, or the money becomes the master of the person. Our Lord uses money to test our lives and as an instrument to mold us into the likeness of Himself."

All through Scripture there is a correlation between the development of people's character and how they handle money. Money is regarded as an index to a person's true character. You have heard the expression, "Money talks," and indeed it does. You can tell a lot about a person's character by examining his or her checkbook and credit card statement because we spend our money on the things that are most important to us.

3. Having Our Finances in Order

As we apply God's principles to our finances, we will begin to get out of debt, spend more wisely, start saving for our future, and give even more to the work of Christ. Following the *Crown Money Map*™ will help you become financially healthy.

PRINCIPLES OF FAITHFULNESS

We can draw important principles of faithfulness from the Lord's parables.

1. If we waste possessions, God may remove us as stewards.

"There was a certain rich man who had a manager [steward], who was reported to him as squandering his possessions. And he called him and said to him, 'What is this I hear about you? Give an account of your management, for you can no longer be [steward]'" (Luke 16:1-2).

IF YOU WASTE THE POS-SESSIONS ENTRUSTED TO YOU, YOU MAY NOT BE GIVEN MORE.

Two principles from this passage are applicable to us. First, when we waste our possessions it becomes public knowledge and creates a poor testimony. *"[The steward] was reported to him as squandering his possessions."* Second, God may remove us as stewards if we squander what He has given to us.

A businessman earned a fortune in just three years and then went on a spending spree. Two years later he informed his office staff that he had little left and everyone would need to economize. Shortly thereafter, he left for an expensive vacation and had his office completely renovated at a cost of thousands of dollars. God soon removed this man from the privilege of being steward over much, and today he is on the verge of bankruptcy.

If you waste the possessions entrusted to you, you may not be given more.

2. We must be faithful in little things.

"He who is faithful in a very little thing is faithful also in much; and he who is unrighteous in a very little thing is unrighteous also in much" (Luke 16:10).

How do you know if your son is going to take good care of his first car? Observe how he cared for his bicycle. How do you know if a salesperson will do a competent job of serving a large client? Evaluate how she serves a small client. If we have the character to be faithful with small things, God knows He can trust us with greater responsibilities. Small things are small things, but faithfulness with a small thing is a big thing.

3. We must be faithful with another's possessions.

Faithfulness with another's possessions in some measure will determine how much you are given. *"If you have not been faithful in the use of that which is another's, who will give you that which is your own?"* (Luke 16:12).

This is a principle that is often overlooked. One of the most faithful men I know rented a vehicle from a friend and damaged it in an accident. He told the owner what happened and then delivered the vehicle to the owner's mechanic with these instructions: "Make it better than it was before the accident, and I will be responsible for the bill." What an example!

When someone allows you to use something, are you careful to return it promptly and in good shape? Are you careless with your employer's office supplies? Do you waste electricity when you are staying in a hotel room? Some people have not been entrusted with more because they have been unfaithful with the possessions of others.

God promises to do His part in our finances; our part is to grow in faithfulness.

Startling Statistics

● *Two of every three middle-income Americans—66 percent—live from paycheck to paycheck.*

MY NOTES

"Just as the rich rule the poor, so the borrower is servant to the lender"

(Proverbs 22:7, TLB).

DEBT

Debt is slavery.

Scripture to Memorize

"Just as the rich rule the poor, so the borrower is servant to the lender" (Proverbs 22:7, TLB).

Practical Application

Complete the Debt List and review Destination 2 on the _Crown Money Map._™

Day One - Let's Review God's Part and Our Part

Read the God's Part/Our Part Notes on pages 18-25 and answer:

1. How have you observed God using money to mold your character?

2. What strengths have been developed in your character?

3. What weaknesses in your character still need to be addressed?

DEBT

Day Two

Read Deuteronomy 15:4-6; Deuteronomy 28:1, 2, 12; and Deuteronomy 28:15, 43-45.

1. According to these passages how was debt viewed in the Old Testament?

2. What was the cause of someone getting in debt (needing to borrow) or being free of debt (able to lend)?

Day Three

Read Romans 13:8; Proverbs 22:7; and 1 Corinthians 7:23.

1. Why is debt discouraged in Scripture?

   Romans 13:8 -

   Proverbs 22:7 -

   1 Corinthians 7:23 -

2. How does this apply to you personally and to your business?

3. If you are in debt, do you have a strategy to get out of debt? If you have a plan, please describe it.

Day Four

Read Psalm 37:21 and Proverbs 3:27-28.

1. What do these verses say about debt repayment?

   Psalm 37:21 -

   Proverbs 3:27-28 -

2. How will you implement this?

Day Five

Read 2 Kings 4:1-7.

1. What principles of getting out of debt can you identify from this passage?

2. Can you apply any of these principles to your present situation? How?

Day Six

Read Proverbs 22:26-27 and Proverbs 17:18.

1. What does the Bible say about cosigning (striking hands, surety)?

  Proverbs 22:26-27 -

  Proverbs 17:18 -

Read Proverbs 6:1-5.

2. If someone has cosigned, what should he or she attempt to do?

☑ Please write your prayer requests in your prayer log before coming to the meeting.

☑ I will take the following action as a result of this week's study:

The amount of debt in our nation has exploded—government debt, business debt, and personal debt. The average household spends $1.10 for every $1 it earns! We are drowning in a sea of debt. More than 1 million individuals a year file bankruptcy. And more sobering, a Gallup Poll found that 56 percent of all divorces are a result of financial tension in the home.

Such financial tension results from believing the "gospel" according to Madison Avenue: Buy now and pay later with easy monthly payments. We all know that nothing about those monthly payments is easy. Advertisers fail to tell us the whole truth. They leave out one little word: debt.

WHAT IS DEBT?

The dictionary defines debt as "money that a person is obligated to pay to another." Debt includes bank loans, money borrowed from relatives, the home mortgage, past-due medical bills, and money owed to credit card companies. Bills that come due, such as the monthly electric bill, are not considered debt if they are paid on time.

WHAT DEBT REALLY COSTS

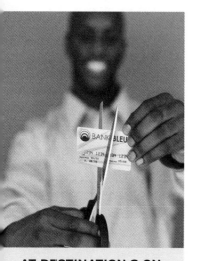

AT DESTINATION 2 ON THE MONEY MAP, YOU FOCUS ON PAYING OFF YOUR CREDIT CARDS.

We need to understand the real cost of debt. Assume you have $5,560 in credit card debt at an 18 percent interest rate. This would cost you $1,000 in interest annually. Study the chart below.

1. Amount of interest you paid

Year 5	Year 10	Year 20	Year 30	Year 40
$5,000	$10,000	$20,000	$30,000	$40,000

2. What you would accumulate on $1,000 invested annually earning 12 percent

Year 5	Year 10	Year 20	Year 30	Year 40
$6,353	$17,549	$72,052	$241,333	$767,091

3. How much the lender earns from your interest payment at 18 percent interest

Year 5	Year 10	Year 20	Year 30	Year 40
$7,154	$23,521	$146,628	$790,948	$4,163,213

You can see what lenders have known for a long time: the incredible impact of compounding interest working for them. If they earn 18 percent, they will accumulate more than $4 million on your $1,000 a year for 40 years! Is there any wonder credit card companies are eager for you to become one of their borrowers?

Now compare the $40,000 you paid in interest over 40 years with the $767,091 you would have accumulated if you earned 12 percent on $1,000 each year. The monthly income on $767,091 earning 12 percent—without ever touching the principal—is $7,671!

Debt has a much higher cost than many realize. Stop to consider this: When you assume debt of $5,560 and pay $1,000 a year in interest versus earning a 12 percent return on that $1000, it actually costs you $767,091 over 40 years. The next time you are tempted to purchase something with debt, ask yourself if the long-term benefits of staying out of debt outweigh the short-term benefits of the purchase.

The Other Costs of Debt

Debt often increases stress, which contributes to mental, physical, and emotional fatigue. It can stifle creativity and harm relationships. Many people raise their lifestyle through debt, only to discover that its burden then controls their lifestyle.

THE BIBLE ON DEBT

Scripture does not say that debt is a sin, but it discourages it. Remember, God loves us and has given us these principles for our benefit. Read the first portion of Romans 13:8 from several different translations: *"Owe no man any thing"* (KJV). *"Let no debt remain outstanding"* (NIV). *"Pay all your debts"* (TLB). *"Owe nothing to anyone"* (NASB). *"Keep out of debt and owe no man anything"* (AMPLIFIED).

1. Debt is considered slavery.

Proverbs 22:7 reads: *"Just as the rich rule the poor, so the borrower is servant to the lender"* (TLB). When we are in debt, we're a servant to the lender. And the deeper we are in debt, the more like servants we become. We don't have the freedom to decide where to spend our income because it is already obligated to meet these debts.

In 1 Corinthians 7:23, Paul writes, *"You were bought with a price; do not become slaves of men."* Our Father made the ultimate sacrifice by giving His Son, the Lord Jesus Christ, to die for us. And He now wants His children free to serve Him rather than lenders.

2. Debt was considered a curse.

In the Old Testament, being out of debt was one of the promised rewards for obedience.

> *"If you diligently obey the Lord your God, being careful to do all His commandments which I command you today, the Lord your God will set you high above all the nations of the earth. All these blessings will come upon you. . . . You shall lend to many nations, but you shall not borrow"* (Deuteronomy 28:1-2, 12).

However, debt was one of the curses for disobedience.

> *"If you do not obey the Lord your God, to observe to do all His commandments and His statutes with which I charge you today, that all these curses*

will come upon you and overtake you. . . . The alien who is among you shall rise above you higher and higher, but you will go down lower and lower. He shall lend to you, but you will not lend to him; he shall be the head, and you will be the tail" (Deuteronomy 28:15, 43-44).

3. Debt presumes upon tomorrow.

When we get into debt, we assume that we will earn enough in the future to repay it. We plan for our jobs to continue or our investments to be profitable. The Bible cautions us against presumption: *"You who say, 'Today or tomorrow, we shall go to such and such a city, and spend a year there and engage in business and make a profit.' Yet you do not know what your life will be like tomorrow. . . . Instead, you ought to say, 'If the Lord wills, we shall live and also do this or that'"* (James 4:13-15).

4. Debt may deny God an opportunity.

Ron Blue, an outstanding financial author, tells of a young man who wanted to go to seminary to become a missionary. The young man had no money and thought the only way he could afford seminary was to secure a student loan. However, this would have left him with $40,000 of debt by the time he graduated. He knew a missionary's salary would never be able to repay that much debt.

After a great deal of prayer, he decided to enroll without the aid of a loan, trusting God to meet his needs. He graduated without borrowing anything and grew in his appreciation for how God could provide his needs. This was the most valuable lesson learned in seminary as he prepared for life on the mission field.

BORROWING

The Bible is silent on when we can owe money. In our opinion it is permissible to owe money for a home mortgage, your business or vocation. This "permissible debt" should meet three criteria.

- The item purchased is an asset with the potential to appreciate or produce an income.
- The value of an item exceeds the amount owed against it.
- The debt should not be so high that repayment puts undue strain on the spending plan.

Here's how a home mortgage might qualify. Houses meet the first requirement since they usually appreciate. You can meet the second requirement by investing a reasonable down payment so that you could expect to sell the home for at least enough to pay off the mortgage. The third requirement means buying an affordable house—one with a monthly payment that doesn't strain your spending plan.

If you take on some debt, we pray you will establish the goal of immediately eliminating it.

HOW TO GET OUT OF DEBT

Consider these nine steps for getting out of debt. The steps are easy, but following them requires discipline. The goal is D-Day—Debtless Day—when you become absolutely free of debt.

1. Pray.

In 2 Kings 4:1-7, we read about a widow who was threatened with losing her sons to her creditor. When she asked Elisha for help, he told her to borrow many empty jars from her neighbors. Then God multiplied her only possession—a small amount of oil—until all the jars were filled. She sold the oil and paid her debts to free her children.

The same God who provided supernaturally for the widow is interested in freeing you from debt. The first step is to pray. Seek God's help and guidance in your journey toward Debtless Day. He may act immediately or slowly over time. In either case, prayer is essential. A trend is emerging. As people begin to eliminate debt, the Lord blesses their faithfulness. Even if you can afford only a small monthly prepayment of your debt, please do it. God can multiply your efforts.

2. Sell what you are not using.

Evaluate your possessions to determine whether you should sell any of them to help you get out of debt more quickly. What about the clothes you no longer wear? That set of golf clubs gathering dust? Is there anything you can sell to help you get out of debt?

3. Decide which debts to pay off first by following the Crown Money Map.

At Destination 2 on the Money Map, you focus on paying off your credit cards because they usually have the highest interest rate. At Destination 3, you will wipe out your consumer debt: car loans, student loans, home equity loans, medical debts, and so forth. And at Destination 5, you begin to accelerate the payment of your home mortgage.

4. The Snowball Strategy.

How do you "snowball" yourself out of debt?

- **Pay off your smallest credit card debt.**
  Review your credit card debts. In addition to making the minimum payments on all your cards, focus on accelerating the payment of your smallest high-interest credit card first. You will be encouraged as you make progress, finally eliminating that debt.
- **After you pay off the first credit card, apply its payment toward the next smallest one.** After the second card is paid off, apply what you were paying on the first and second toward the third smallest credit card, and so forth. That's the snowball strategy in action!
- **Pay off your smallest consumer debt.**
  After you have paid off all your credit cards, focus on paying off your consumer debts in exactly the same way as you wiped out your plastic. Make

the minimum payments on all your consumer debts, but focus on accelerating the payment of your smallest higher-interest consumer debt first. Then, after you pay off the first consumer debt, apply its payment toward the next smallest one. After the second one is paid off, apply what you were paying on the first and second to pay off the third, and so forth.

5. Consider earning additional income.

Many people hold jobs that simply do not pay enough to allow them to pay off their debts quickly enough. A temporary part-time job can make a huge difference in how fast you reach D-Day.

6. Control the use of the plastic.

A wave of credit card solicitations is overwhelming our mailboxes. Many of these entice us with low teaser rates that rise to high levels within a few months. Credit cards are not sinful, but they are dangerous.

One way to limit the temptations of additional cards and to make mealtime more peaceful is to opt out of receiving telemarketing calls and pre-approved credit card offers by mail. Log on the Web site of the National Do Not Call Registry at DoNotCall.gov to stop telemarketers. To stop junk mail, call toll free 1-(888)-5OPT-OUT. Everyone should do this!

When people use credit cards rather than cash, they spend about one-third more because it doesn't feel like real money; it's just plastic. As one shopper said to another, "I like credit cards lots more than money, because they go so much further!" If you don't pay the entire credit card balance at the end of each month, you may need to perform some plastic surgery—any good scissors will do!

7. Be content with what you have.

Advertisers use powerful methods to get us to buy. Frequently the message is intended to foster discontentment with what we have. An example is the American company that opened a new plant in Central America because the labor was relatively inexpensive. Everything went well until the villagers received their first paycheck; afterward they did not return to work. Several days later, the manager went down to the village chief to determine the cause of this problem. The chief responded, "Why should we work? We already have everything we need." The plant stood idle for two months until someone came up with the idea of sending a mail-order catalog to every villager. There has not been an employment problem since!

Note these three realities of our consumer-driven economy.

- The more television you watch or surfing the Web you do, the more you spend.
- The more you look at catalogs and magazines, the more you spend.
- The more you shop, the more you spend.

There is an interesting passage in 1 Timothy 6:5-6: "... *Men of depraved mind and deprived of the truth ... suppose that godliness is a means of gain. But godliness actually is a means of great gain when accompanied by contentment.*" When we are content with what we have and wait to buy until we can do it using cash—that is great gain.

8. Consider a radical change in lifestyle.

A growing number of people have lowered their standard of living significantly to get out of debt more quickly. Some have downsized their homes, rented apartments, or moved in with family members. Many have sold cars with large monthly payments and have bought inexpensive ones for cash. In short, they have temporarily sacrificed their standard of living so they could snowball their debt more quickly.

9. Do not give up!

The last step may be the most difficult. On October 29, 1941, Winston Churchill, Prime Minister of England, gave a commencement address. World War II was devastating Europe, and England's fate was in doubt. Churchill stood and said, "Never give in. Never give in. Never, never, never, never—in nothing, great or small, large or petty—never give in except to convictions of honor and good sense."

Never give up in your effort to get out of debt. It may require hard work and sacrifice, but the freedom is worth the struggle.

ESCAPING THE AUTO DEBT TRAP

Car debt is one of the biggest obstacles for most people on their journey to true financial freedom because most people never get out of it. Just when they are ready to pay off a car, they trade it in and purchase a newer one with credit.

Unlike a home, which usually appreciates in value, the moment you drive a car off the lot it depreciates in value. It's worth less than you paid for it.

Take these three steps to get out of auto debt:

1. Decide to keep your car at least three years longer than your car loan and pay off your car loan.
2. After your last payment, keep making the payment, but pay it to yourself. Put it into an account that you will use to buy your next car.
3. When you are ready to replace your car, the cash you have saved plus your car's trade-in value should be sufficient to buy a car without credit. It may not be a new car, but a newer low-mileage used car without any debt is a better value anyway.

THE HOME MORTGAGE

If you own a home or plan to purchase one in the future, we want to encourage you to pay it off more rapidly than scheduled.

When my wife, Bev, and I first learned God's financial principles, we decided to work toward paying off everything, including the home mortgage. Frankly, this was a pipe dream for us at the time, but we began to explore how we might do it.

Understanding the numbers

Every mortgage comes with a payment schedule based on the length of the loan and the interest rate. Knowing how this works will help you develop a plan for paying off the mortgage. Let's examine the payment schedule of a mortgage.

HeyHoward@Crown.org

Q: *Should we sell our home and pay off our credit cards and car loans so that we can complete the Money Map destinations in order?*

A: It all depends. If you live in an affordable home and can make steady progress on the Money Map, keep it. However, if you home is too expensive and stretches your spending plan to the breaking point, consider downsizing.

In the example below, we are assuming a $150,000 mortgage at a 7.5 percent fixed interest rate, paid over 30 years. The first year looks like this:

PAYMENT SCHEDULE

Paymt. #	Month	Payment	Interest	Principal	Balance
0					$150,000.00
1	Jan	$1,048.82	$937.50	$111.32	$149,888.68
2	Feb	$1,048.82	$936.80	$112.02	$149,776.66
3	Mar	$1,048.82	$936.10	$112.72	$149,663.94
4	Apr	$1,048.82	$935.40	$113.42	$149,550.52
5	May	$1,048.82	$934.69	$114.13	$149,436.39
6	Jun	$1,048.82	$933.98	$114.84	$149,321.55
7	Jul	$1,048.82	$933.26	$115.56	$149,205.98
8	Aug	$1,048.82	$932.54	$116.28	$149,089.70
9	Sep	$1,048.82	$931.81	$117.01	$148,972.69
10	Oct	$1,048.82	$931.08	$117.74	$148,854.95
11	Nov	$1,048.82	$930.34	$118.48	$148,736.47
12	Dec	$1,048.82	$929.60	$119.22	$148,617.25

Totals for year: $12,585.84 $11,203.11 $1,382.73

As you can see, the payments during the first year are largely interest. Of the $12,585.84 in payments, only $1,382.73 will go toward principal reduction. In fact, it will be 23 years before the principal and interest portions of the payment will equal each other!

Now here's something really important to remember. Interest is charged on the remaining unpaid principal balance. Look at the schedule above.

In January, if you paid your first monthly payment of $1,048.82 plus the next month's principal payment of $112.02, the principal balance would be $149,776.66. So in February when you make your regular payment of $1,048.82, it is applied as though it were payment #3. Now, look carefully at payment #2. You paid $112.02 extra and saved the $936.80 in interest you would have paid. That is a great deal! Can you see why I hope that you will catch the vision of paying off your home? There's nothing magical about what I'm suggesting. Once you understand how it works, the numbers will work for you.

How to Pay Off the Mortgage More Quickly

There are several ways to accelerate the payment of your home mortgage.

1. Reduce the length of the mortgage.

If you need a new mortgage or the conditions are favorable for you to refinance, consider a shorter-term mortgage. If you can afford higher payments, go with a 15-year instead of a 30-year mortgage. The interest rate on a 15-year mortgage is normally lower than the 30-year rate, and the outstanding balance shrinks much faster.

Let's compare a $150,000, 30-year mortgage at 7.5 percent and a 15-year mortgage at 7 percent.

Total Mortgage $150,000	Thirty Years	Fifteen Years
Monthly Payment	$1,048	$1,348
At the end of fifteen years:		
Interest paid	$151,928	$92,683
Principal paid	$36,859	$150,000
Principal Balance Due	$131,140	$0 (Yes!)
Interest paid, years 15-30	$75,649	$0
Total interest paid	**$227,577**	**$92,683**

If you can shrink the duration of your mortgage in half, the savings in interest is huge.

2. Add something to the required payment.

You can still accelerate the repayment of your mortgage simply by paying an extra amount each month or as frequently as possible. That's what Bev and I did. We started small. Each month we put a little more on the mortgage to reduce the principal more quickly. The longer we did it, the more excited we became.

3. Bonuses and tax returns.

Finally, when you receive a work bonus or an income tax refund, give generously to God and then consider applying the rest to your home mortgage. Doing that each time it occurs can have a significant impact on paying off your home.

I remember receiving an unexpected bonus. Instead of taking a vacation or buying something, we applied it toward the mortgage. That bonus alone allowed us to shorten our mortgage by several years.

There are three primary arguments against prepaying a mortgage. (1) Why pay off a low-interest home mortgage when you can earn more elsewhere? (2) With inflation, your later payments are made with less valuable dollars. (3) You lose a tax shelter because the interest paid on a home mortgage is tax deductible.

Rather than take the time to address these arguments, we should recognize that the tax system in America is designed to reward indebtedness. We get a tax break for interest paid on our home mortgage. However, the Bible discourages debt. We simply challenge you to seek Christ with an open heart to learn what He wants you to do.

For Bev and me, this turned into an exciting time as we began to pay off our mortgage. The Lord provided additional funds for us in an unexpected way, and today we do not owe anyone anything. This allowed me to take the time to develop the Crown materials. God may have something similar for you.

Let me ask you a question: How would it feel to have no debt and no payments of any kind including your home mortgage? We can tell you from experience, it feels great!

If you want to pay off your mortgage, it is a good idea to inform your lender of your plans, to ensure proper crediting of your prepayment.

HOW WOULD IT FEEL TO HAVE NO DEBT AND NO PAYMENTS OF ANY KIND?

INVESTMENT DEBT

Should you borrow money to make an investment? In our opinion, it is permissible to borrow for an investment, but only if the investment (along with your down payment) is the sole collateral for the debt. You should not personally guarantee repayment of the debt. At first, this may appear to contradict the biblical admonition to repay our debts. But let's explore this issue further.

Suppose you wanted to purchase a rental property with a reasonable down payment, making sure that the house would be the sole security for the debt. You would explain to potential lenders that at your option, you would repay the loan in one of two ways: First, by giving the lender cash—making the payments. Or second, by giving the lender the property plus the down payment and any other money you had invested in the house.

Given those options, the lender must make a decision. Is the down payment sufficient? Is the house of adequate value? Is the real estate market strong enough for the lender to feel secure about making the loan?

Some investors have responded that it is impossible to locate a lender willing to loan without a personal guarantee. However, when I was in the real estate business, I prayed for this type of financing and then knocked on lots of doors. Eventually I got it. Some of the loans came from owners selling their properties, some came from lending institutions.

Because of the possibility of difficult financial events over which you have no control, be sure to limit your potential loss to the cash you invest and the asset itself. It is painful to lose your investment, but it is much more serious to jeopardize your family's needs by risking all your personal assets on investment debt. What we're suggesting may appear too conservative, but many people have become slaves of the lender and lost everything by guaranteeing debt on investments that went sour.

BUSINESS DEBT

We also want to encourage you to pray about becoming debt free in your business. Many business owners are recognizing the competitive advantage and increased stability they have when they eliminate business debt.

Here is our rule of thumb on business debt: Use as little as possible and pay it off as quickly as possible.

CHURCH DEBT

Scripture does not specifically address whether a church may borrow money to build or expand its facility. In our opinion, such debt is permissible if the church leadership clearly senses the Lord leading to do so. If a church borrows, we recommend that it raise as much money as possible for the down payment and establish a plan to pay off the debt as rapidly as possible. A growing number of churches have chosen to build without the use of any debt. For many of these churches, the members have been encouraged and their faith increased as they have observed God providing the necessary funds.

REPAYMENT RESPONSIBILITIES

PROMPT PAYMENT

Many people delay paying creditors until payments are past due, even when they have the money. This, however, is not biblical. Proverbs 3:27-28 reads, *"Do not withhold good from those to whom it is due, when it is in your power to do it. Do not say to your neighbor, 'Go, and come back, and tomorrow I will give it,' when you have it with you."*

Godly people should pay their debts and bills as promptly as they can. Some try to pay each bill the same day they receive it to demonstrate to others that knowing Jesus Christ has made them financially responsible.

USING YOUR SAVINGS

In our opinion, it's not smart to use all your savings to pay off debt. Follow the *Crown Money Map*™ and keep three months living expenses set aside for emergencies.

BANKRUPTCY

A court can declare people bankrupt and unable to pay their debts. Depending on the type of bankruptcy, the court will either allow them to develop a plan to repay their creditors or it will distribute their property among the creditors as payment.

Should a godly person declare bankruptcy? Generally, no. Psalm 37:21 tells us, *"The wicked borrows and does not pay back."*

However, in our opinion, bankruptcy is permissible under three circumstances:

- A creditor forces a person into bankruptcy.
- The borrower experiences such extreme financial difficulties that there is no option. There are occasions when bankruptcy is the only viable option when the financial challenges become too extreme to reverse. That option needs to be exercised only after all others have been explored.
- The emotional health of the borrower is at stake. If the debtor's emotional health is at stake because of inability to cope with the pressure of aggressive creditors, bankruptcy can be an option.

Declaring bankruptcy should not be a cavalier decision, because it remains on a credit report for 10 years, and it often impairs ones ability to obtain future credit at reasonable interest rates. Potential employers and landlords are also likely to learn of a past bankruptcy. It can haunt people for some time, and although it provides relief, it is not exactly the fresh start that some advertise.

COSIGNING

Cosigning relates to debt. Anytime you cosign, you become legally responsible for the debt of another. It is just as if you went to the bank, borrowed the money and gave it to your friend or relative who is asking you to cosign. In effect, you promise to pay back the entire amount if the borrower does not.

A Federal Trade Commission study found that 50 percent of those who cosigned for bank loans ended up making the payments. And 75 percent of those who cosigned for finance company loans ended up making the payments! Those are pretty good odds that if you cosign, you'll pay. The casualty rate is so high because the professional lender knows the loan is a bad risk and told himself, I won't touch this loan with a 10-foot pole unless I can get someone who is financially responsible to guarantee its repayment.

Fortunately, Scripture gives us clear direction about cosigning. Proverbs 17:18 says, *"It is poor judgment to countersign another's note, to become responsible for his debts"* (TLB). The words "poor judgment" are literally translated "destitute of mind"!

A parent often cosigns for his or her child's first automobile. The Watsons decided not to do this. They wanted to model for their children the importance of not cosigning and to discourage them from using debt. Instead, they trained them to think ahead and save for the cash purchase of their first cars.

If you have already cosigned for a loan, the Scripture gives you counsel. Proverbs 6:1-5 says, *"Son, if you endorse a note for someone you hardly know, guaranteeing his debt, you are in serious trouble. You may have trapped yourself by your agreement. Quick! Get out of it if you possibly can! Swallow your pride; don't let embarrassment stand in the way. Go and beg to have your name erased. Don't put it off. . . . If you can get out of this trap you have saved yourself like a deer that escapes from a hunter, or a bird from the net"* (TLB).

Please use sound judgment and never cosign.

CREDIT REPORT AND SCORE

Everyone should get a copy of their credit report once every 12 months. To order a free copy, log on to AnnualCreditReport.com.

Your credit score (FICO score) determines whether you can get credit. And your score may be high enough to get credit but not high enough to get a decent interest rate—whether you're looking for a mortgage, a credit card, a car loan, or some other type of credit. Without good scores, your application to rent an apartment may be turned down. Your scores can affect your car insurance premiums and in some cases even getting a job.

A credit score is a number designed to help lenders and others measure your likelihood of making payments on time. The score ranges from 300-850. Higher scores are better—scores above 700 indicate a good credit risk, while scores below 600 indicate a poor risk.

A low score can lead to much higher interest rates. For example, if you apply for a 30-year home mortgage and your credit score is too low, you could pay as much as 3 percent more. On a $100,000 mortgage, that 3 percent difference will cost you $200 per month. Over the life of the loan it adds up to $72,000!

The primary things that will harm your credit score are late payments or non-payments of bills or debts, bankruptcy, foreclosure, repossession, bills or loans sent to collection. Your credit score will also be affected if your credit history is short, or if you have maxed out your credit limits. To improve your credit score, the two most important actions you can take are to pay your bills on time and to reduce your total debt. Once you start doing this, your score will begin to improve in about three months.

MY NOTES

*"The way of a fool is right in his own eyes,
but a wise man is he who listens to counsel"*
(Proverbs 12:15).

COUNSEL

*A wise person
seeks advice.*

TO BE COMPLETED <u>PRIOR TO</u> WEEK 4 MEETING

 Scripture to Memorize

"The way of a fool is right in his own eyes, but a wise man is he who listens to counsel" (Proverbs 12:15).

 Practical Application

Complete the Estimated Spending Plan and the Spending Plan Analysis, and review Destination 3 on the *Crown Money Map.™*

Day One - Let's Review Debt

Read the Debt Notes on pages 32-42 and answer:

1. Are you in debt? If so, what steps do you sense God wants you to take to become free of debt?

2. What did you learn about debt that proved to be especially helpful?

COUNSEL

Day Two

Read Proverbs 12:15; Proverbs 13:10; and Proverbs 15:22.

1. What are some of the benefits of seeking counsel?

    Proverbs 12:15 –

    Proverbs 13:10 –

    Proverbs 15:22 –

2. What are some of the benefits you have experienced from seeking counsel?

3. What hinders you from seeking counsel?

Day Three

Read Psalm 16:7 and Psalm 32:8.

1. In what ways does God actively counsel His children?

Read Psalm 106:13-15.

2. What was the consequence of not seeking the Lord's counsel in this passage?

3. Have you ever suffered for not seeking God's counsel? If so, describe what happened.

Day Four

Read Psalm 119:24; Psalm 119:105; 2 Timothy 3:16-17; and Hebrews 4:12.

1. Give several reasons why the Bible should serve as your counselor.

Read Psalm 119:98-100.

2. Living by the counsel of Scripture –

    Makes us wiser than:

    Gives us more insight than:

    Gives us more understanding than:

3. Do you consistently read and study the Bible? If not, what prevents your consistency?

Day Five

Read Proverbs 1:8-9.

1. Who should be among your counselors?

2. In your opinion, who should be the number-one human counselor of a husband? Of a wife? Why?

Read Proverbs 11:14 and Ecclesiastes 4:9-12.

3. What do these verses communicate to you?

    Proverbs 11:14 –

    Ecclesiastes 4:9-12 –

4. How do you propose to apply this principle in your personal and/or business life?

Day Six

Read Psalm 1:1-3.

1. Whom should you avoid as a counselor?

2. What is your definition of a wicked person?

Read Proverbs 12:5.

3. Why should you avoid their counsel?

4. Is there ever a circumstance in which you should seek the input of a person who does not know Christ? If so, when?

Follow-up

☑ Please write your prayer requests in your prayer log before coming to the meeting.

☑ I will take the following action as a result of this week's study:

I frequently counsel people with financial problems. Often they could have avoided their difficulties if only they had sought counsel from someone with a solid understanding of God's way of handling money.

SEEKING COUNSEL

Two attitudes keep us from seeking counsel. The first one is pride. Our culture perceives seeking advice as a sign of weakness. We are told, "Stand on your own two feet. You don't need anyone to help make your decisions for you!" Advertisers subtly encourage this because they know that the impulse sale is often lost when the purchaser takes time to seek counsel.

The second attitude is stubbornness, characterized by the statement, "Don't confuse me with the facts. My mind is already made up!" We often resist seeking counsel because we do not want to learn the financial facts another person might discover. We don't want to be told we can't afford what we already have decided to buy.

God encourages us to use a great gift He has provided for our benefit—godly counselors. In Proverbs 19:20 we read, *"Listen to advice and accept instruction, and in the end you will be wise"* (NIV). Proverbs 12:15 says, *"The way of a fool is right in his own eyes, but a wise man is he who listens to counsel."* And Proverbs 10:8 says, *"The wise man is glad to be instructed, but a self-sufficient fool falls flat on his face"* (TLB).

We seek counsel to secure insights, suggestions, and alternatives that will aid in making a proper decision. It is not the counselor's role to make the decision; we retain that responsibility.

Gather facts, but. . . .

We need to assemble the facts that will influence our decisions, but we also need to seek God's direction as well. Sometimes He directs in a way contrary to our assessment of the facts alone.

This is illustrated in Numbers 13 and 14. Moses sent 12 spies into the Promised Land. They all returned with an identical evaluation of the facts: It was a prosperous land inhabited by terrifying giants. Only two of the 12 spies, Joshua and Caleb, understood God wanted them to go in and possess the Promised Land. Because the children of Israel relied only on the facts and did not act in faith on what the Lord wanted for them, they suffered 40 years of wandering in the wilderness until that entire generation died.

IF YOU ARE MARRIED, THE FIRST PERSON YOU NEED TO CONSULT IS YOUR SPOUSE.

SOURCES OF COUNSEL

What are the sources of counsel we need to seek? Before making a financial decision, particularly an important one, subject it to three sources of counsel.

THE COUNSEL OF SCRIPTURE

First, what does God's Word say about a particular issue? The Psalmist wrote, *"Your laws are both my light and my counselors"* (Psalm 119:24, TLB).

"Your commands make me wiser than my enemies. . . . I have more insight than all my teachers, for I meditate on your statutes" (Psalm 119:98-99, NIV). *"I understand more than the aged, because I have observed Your precepts"* (Psalm 119:100).

When we think of people who are skilled in financial decision making, we often think of experts or those who are older and more experienced. Yet the Bible offers us more insight and wisdom than financial experts who do not know God's way of handling money. I would rather obey the truth of Scripture than risk suffering the consequences of following my own inclinations or the opinions of people.

The Bible makes this remarkable claim about itself: *"For the word of God is living and active and sharper than any two-edged sword, and . . . able to judge the thoughts and intentions of the heart"* (Hebrews 4:12). The truths in the Bible are timeless. It is a living book that communicates God's direction to all generations.

You may have been surprised to learn that the Bible contains 2,350 verses dealing with how we should handle money and possessions. It is the very first filter through which we should run a financial decision. If it answers the question, we do not have to go any further because the Bible contains God's written, revealed will.

Bob and Barbara faced a difficult choice. Barbara's brother and his wife had just moved from Chicago to Florida. Because they had experienced financial difficulties in Chicago, the bank would not give them a home loan unless they had someone cosign the debt. They asked Bob and Barbara, and although Barbara pleaded for Bob to cosign, he was reluctant.

A friend referred them to the verses that warn against cosigning. After reading the passages, Barbara said, "Who am I to argue with God? We shouldn't cosign." Bob was tremendously relieved.

Two years later, Barbara's brother and his wife were divorced, and he declared bankruptcy. Can you imagine the strain on their marriage if Bob had cosigned? He might have said, "Barbara, I can't believe your brother did this! You got me into this! I tried not to cosign but you forced me!" They probably would not have been able to survive financially.

If the Bible provides clear direction in a financial matter, we know what to do. If the Bible is not specific about an issue, we should subject our decision to the second source of counsel: godly people.

> **IF THE BIBLE PROVIDES CLEAR DIRECTION IN A FINANCIAL MATTER, WE KNOW WHAT TO DO.**

THE COUNSEL OF GODLY PEOPLE

"The godly man is a good counselor because he is just and fair and knows right from wrong" (Psalm 37:30-31, TLB). The Christian life is not one of independence from other Christians but of interdependence on one other. This is illustrated clearly in Paul's discussion concerning the body of Christ in 1 Corinthians 12. Each of us is pictured as a different member of this body. Our ability to function most effectively is dependent on the members working together. God has given each of us certain abilities and gifts, but God has not given any one person all the abilities that he or she needs to be most productive.

Spouse

If you are married, the first person you need to consult is your spouse. Frankly, it has been a humbling experience for me to seek the counsel of my wife, Bev, in financial matters because she has no formal financial training. But she has saved us a great deal of money by her wise counsel.

Women tend to be gifted with a wonderfully sensitive and intuitive nature that is usually very accurate. Men tend to focus more objectively on the facts. The husband and wife need each other to achieve the proper balance for a correct decision. I believe that the Lord honors the wife's "office" or "position" as helpmate to her husband. Many times God communicates most clearly to the husband through his wife.

If you are a husband, let me be blunt. Regardless of her business background or her financial aptitude, you must cultivate and seek your wife's counsel. I have committed never to proceed with a financial decision unless Bev agrees. There are additional benefits from seeking your spouse's counsel.

- **It will preserve your relationship!**

   The husband and wife should agree, because they both will experience the consequences of the decision. Even if their choice proves to be disastrous, their relationship remains intact. There are no grounds for an "I told you so" response.

- **It honors your spouse.**

   Unfortunately, some in our culture do not feel valuable. Seeking your spouse's counsel will help enormously in the development of a healthy and proper self-esteem. When a husband or wife seeks the other's advice, he or she actually is communicating, "I love you. I respect you. I value your insight."

- **It prepares your spouse for the future.**

   Consistently asking for advice also keeps your spouse informed of your true financial condition. This is important in the event you predecease your spouse or are unable to work. My father suffered a massive heart attack that incapacitated him for two years. Because he kept my mother informed about his business, she was able to step in and operate it successfully until he recovered.

Parents

The second source of counsel is our parents.

"My son, observe the commandment of your father and do not forsake the teaching of your mother; bind them continually on your heart; tie them around your neck. When you walk about, they will guide you; when you sleep, they will watch over you; and when you awake, they will talk to you" (Proverbs 6:20-22).

Our parents have the benefit of years of experience, and they know us well. In our opinion, we should seek their counsel even if they do not yet know Christ or have not been wise money managers themselves. Over the years, it's not uncommon for a barrier to be erected between a child and parents. Asking their advice is a way to honor our parents and to build a bridge. It is a compliment, an expression of admiration, for anyone to ask your advice. A word of caution: Although the husband and wife should seek the counsel of their parents, the advice of the parents should be subordinate to the advice of the spouse, especially if a family conflict materializes.

"A man shall leave his father and his mother, and shall be joined to his wife; and they shall become one flesh" (Genesis 2:24, NIV).

Christian Financial Advisors

Your financial advisor's worldview is of critical importance because, ultimately, all good financial advice has its root in biblical wisdom. Only a Christian financial advisor equipped to deliver biblical wisdom can offer advice and counsel consistent with the values and priorities of a believer. However, one of the greatest unrecognized and unmet needs in the body of Christ today is the ability to find a competent and capable financial advisor who shares a biblical perspective on financial decisions.

Kingdom Advisors, led by Ron Blue and founded by Larry Burkett, is devoted to equipping Christian financial advisors to apply biblical wisdom to their advice and counsel. Kingdom Advisors leaves to other certification organizations the provision of designations regarding an advisor's technical training in his or her profession. As part of their unique mission, however, Kingdom Advisors has created the Qualified Kingdom Advisor™ designation to provide assurance that a particular advisor has participated in the Kingdom Advisors education program, has met certain ongoing continuing education and ethics requirements, and has committed to incorporating biblical wisdom into his or her financial advice.

The financial advisors eligible to seek the Qualified Kingdom Advisor™ designation include those in the core financial disciplines, including financial planners, investment professionals, attorneys, accountant/tax professionals, insurance professionals and mortgage professionals. To learn more about the organization and the Qualified Kingdom Advisor™ designation, please visit KingdomAdvisors.org.

Experienced People

We should also consult people experienced in the area in which we are attempting to make a decision. If you are considering a real estate investment, locate the most qualified real estate investor to counsel you. If you want to purchase a car, first ask a trustworthy mechanic to examine it and give you an opinion.

A Multitude of Counselors

We read in Proverbs 15:22, *"Without consultation, plans are frustrated, but with many counselors they succeed."* And Proverbs 11:14 says, *"Where there is no guidance the people fall, but in abundance of counselors there is victory."*

I meet regularly with a life group who share their lives with one another and pray for each other. The members of this group know each other well. Over the years, each person has experienced a difficult circumstance or had to make a major decision. We have learned that when someone suffers a painful circumstance, it is difficult to make wise, dispassionate decisions. We have experienced the benefits and safety of having a group of people who love one another and can give objective counsel even if it hurts.

"A CORD OF THREE STRANDS IS NOT QUICKLY TORN APART."

We are more receptive to constructive criticism when it comes from someone who cares for us.

We also have learned that a major advantage of this close relationship is knowing each other's weaknesses and strengths. This knowledge improves our discernment and counsel. Solomon describes the benefits of interdependence upon one another:

> "Two are better than one because they have a good return for their labor. For if either of them falls, the one will lift up his companion. But woe to the one who falls when there is not another to lift him up. . . . And if one can overpower him who is alone, two can resist him. A cord of three strands is not quickly torn apart" (Ecclesiastes 4:9-12).

It can be very productive to gather your counselors together because the suggestions of one will trigger insights from another and clear direction often emerges.

When seeking a multitude of counselors, don't expect them all to offer the same recommendations. They may even disagree sharply, but a common thread usually develops. Other times, each counselor may supply a different insight you need to help you make the decision. We encourage you to include your pastor among your counselors, particularly when you face a major decision.

THROUGHOUT SCRIPTURE WE ARE ENCOURAGED TO WAIT ON THE LORD.

THE COUNSEL OF THE LORD

During the process of analyzing the facts, searching the Bible, and obtaining the counsel of godly people, we need to seek direction from the Lord. This is the most important thing we can do. In Isaiah 9:6 we are told that one of God's names is "Wonderful Counselor."

The Psalms also identify God as our counselor. "I [the Lord] will instruct you and teach you in the way which you should go; I will counsel you with My eye upon you" (Psalm 32:8). "You [the Lord] guide me with your counsel" (Psalm 73:24, NIV). "I will bless the Lord who has counseled me" (Psalm 16:7).

The Bible contains numerous examples of the unfortunate consequences of not seeking God's counsel as well as the blessings of heeding His counsel. After the children of Israel began their campaign to capture the Promised Land, some of the natives (Gibeonites) attempted to enter into a peace treaty with Israel. The Gibeonites deceived the leaders of Israel into believing they were from a distant land. Joshua 9:14-15 reads, "The men of Israel took some of their [Gibeonites'] provisions, and **did not ask for the counsel of the Lord**. Joshua made peace with them and made a covenant with them, to let them live" [emphasis mine].

The consequence of not seeking the Lord's counsel was that the Promised Land remained populated with ungodly people and Israel became ensnared by their false gods. The leaders were influenced by the "facts" they could see—facts that were designed to deceive them into thinking that the Gibeonites lived far away. In many situations, only God can reveal truth and proper direction. Only He knows the future and the ultimate outcome of a decision.

Throughout Scripture we are encouraged to wait on the Lord. Whenever you feel hurried or pressured or confused concerning a decision, go to a quiet place that will allow you to listen for His still, small voice. The world around you screams "Hurry!" but our loving heavenly Father's advice is worth waiting for.

COUNSEL TO AVOID

AVOIDING THE COUNSEL OF THE WICKED

We need to avoid one particular source of counsel. *"How blessed is the man who does not walk in the counsel of the wicked"* (Psalm 1:1). The word "blessed" literally means to be "happy many times over." The definition of a "wicked" person is one who lives without regard to God. A wicked person can be one who does not yet personally know the Lord or one who knows Jesus Christ as Savior but is not following Him in obedience. Avoid the counsel of the wicked.

In our opinion, when you are searching for facts or technical expertise you may seek input from those who are knowledgeable in that area whether they know Christ or not. Then after considering their input, you are responsible to make the final decision.

Fortune Tellers, Mediums, and Spiritualists

The Bible clearly forbids seeking the advice of fortune tellers, mediums, or spiritualists: *"Do not turn to mediums or seek out spiritists, for you will be defiled by them. I am the Lord your God"* (Leviticus 19:31, NIV). Study this next passage carefully: *"Saul died because he was unfaithful to the Lord . . . and even consulted a medium for guidance and did not inquire of the Lord. So the Lord put him to death"* (1 Chronicles 10:13-14, NIV). Saul died, in part, because he went to a medium. We should also avoid anything they use in forecasting the future, such as horoscopes and all other practices of the occult.

Biased Counsel

We need to be cautious of the counsel of the biased. When receiving financial advice, ask yourself these questions: "What stake does this person have in the outcome of my decision? Does he or she stand to gain or lose from this decision?" If the advisor will profit, be cautious when evaluating this counsel and always seek a second, unbiased opinion.

A WORD TO THE COUNSELED

When you are seeking advice, supply your counselor with all the important facts. Do not attempt to manipulate your advisor to give the answer you want by concealing information.

Major Decisions

Whenever you face a major decision such as a job change or home purchase, it is very helpful to go to a quiet place where you can spend uninterrupted time praying, reading Scripture, and seeking God's direction. We encourage you to consider fasting during this time.

Know Your Counselors

Be selective in choosing your counselors. Include those who are gifted with wisdom. *"He who walks with the wise grows wise"* (Proverbs 13:20, NIV). Make sure they have the courage to give you advice that may be contrary to your wishes.

HeyHoward@Crown.org

Q: *How often should my husband and I review our spending plan?*

A: Meet at least once a week to pray, review your financial progress, and celebrate the victories. Use this as an opportunity to grow closer together as a couple.

Continually ask God for wisdom. *"If any of you lacks wisdom, let him ask of God, who gives to all . . . and it will be given to him. But let him ask in faith without any doubting"* (James 1:5-6).

As you seek counsel, do not be surprised if the answer comes out of your own mouth. Interacting with others allows you to verbalize thoughts and feelings that you may never have expressed clearly.

A WORD TO COUNSELORS

Counseling others can be a frustrating experience if you misunderstand the proper role of the counselor. Simply stated, counselors should lovingly communicate their understanding of the truth and then leave the results to God. I have sometimes made the mistake of becoming involved emotionally in whether people would act on my recommendations. I discovered that some people are not yet prepared to follow advice. On some occasions, I later discovered that my counsel was flawed. Counselors need to be content, knowing that the Lord is in control of every counseling experience.

Observe Strict Confidentiality

The person seeking advice needs to know that nothing he or she says will be communicated to another person without permission. Only in an environment of trust will there be the candid dialogue that produces successful results.

When You Do Not Know

When you do not know the answer to a question, be careful not to fabricate one. Simply respond: "I do not know." Often people come with problems or circumstances that are outside of our experience. The best way to serve is to refer them to someone who has expertise in their area of need.

"You shall not steal, nor deal falsely, nor lie to one another"

(Leviticus 19:11).

HONESTY

God's standard is absolute.

HOMEWORK

WEEK 5

 ## Scripture to Memorize

"You shall not steal, nor deal falsely, nor lie to one another" (Leviticus 19:11).

 ## Practical Application

Complete the Snowball Strategy, Debt Repayment Schedule, Adjust Your Spending Plan, and review "Things to Do Sooner Than Later" on the destination page of the *Crown Money Map*.™

Day One - Let's Review Counsel

Read the Counsel Notes on pages 50-56 and answer:

1. What elements of God's perspective on counsel especially interested you?

2. Do you actively seek counsel when faced with a major financial decision? If not, how do you propose to do so in the future?

HONESTY

Day Two

Read Leviticus 19:11-13; Deuteronomy 25:13-16; Ephesians 4:25; and 1 Peter 1:15-16.

1. What do these verses communicate to you about God's demand for honesty?

Leviticus 19:11-13 –

Deuteronomy 25:13-16 –

Ephesians 4:25 –

1 Peter 1:15-16 –

2. Are you consistently honest in even the smallest details? If not, what will you do to change?

3. What are two factors that motivate or influence us to act dishonestly?

4. How does this apply to you?

Day Three

Read Exodus 18:21-22.

1. Does the Lord require honesty for leaders? Why?

Read Proverbs 28:16 and Proverbs 29:12.

2. What are the consequences of dishonesty for people in leadership?

Proverbs 28:16 –

Proverbs 29:12 –

3. How does this apply to you?

Day Four

Read Proverbs 14:2.

1. Can you practice dishonesty while fearing (respecting, honoring) God? Why?

Read Proverbs 26:28 and Romans 13:9-10.

2. According to these passages, can you practice dishonesty and still love your neighbor? Why?

Day Five

Read Psalm 15:1-5; Proverbs 12:22; Proverbs 20:7; and Isaiah 33:15-16.

1. What are some of the benefits of honesty?

    Psalm 15:1-5 –

    Proverbs 12:22 –

    Proverbs 20:7 –

    Isaiah 33:15-16 –

Read Proverbs 3:32; Proverbs 13:11; and Proverbs 21:6.

2. What are some of the curses of dishonesty?

    Proverbs 3:32 –

    Proverbs 13:11 –

    Proverbs 21:6 –

Read Exodus 22:1-4; Numbers 5:5-8; and Luke 19:8.

1. What does the Bible say about restitution?

2. If you have acquired anything dishonestly, how will you make restitution?

Read Exodus 23:8; Proverbs 15:27; and Proverbs 29:4.

3. What does Scripture say about bribes?

4. Have you ever been asked to give or take a bribe? If so, describe what happened.

Follow-up

☑ Please write your prayer requests in your prayer log before coming to the meeting.

☑ I will take the following action as a result of this week's study:

All of us have to make daily decisions about whether to handle money honestly. Do you tell the cashier at the store when you receive too much change? Have you ever tried to sell something and been tempted not to tell the whole truth because you might lose the sale?

HONESTY IN SOCIETY

These decisions are more difficult when so many around us act dishonestly. After pumping $15 of gas in my truck, I asked for a receipt. When the attendant handed me a receipt for $20, I pointed out the mistake. His answer? "Oh, just turn it in to your company and you'll make a fast five bucks. After all, that's what a lot of the mailmen around here do."

When I heard that, my heart sank. The verse that came immediately to mind was Judges 17:6, *"Every man did what was right in his own eyes."* People today do the same thing, formulating their own standards of honesty and then changing them when circumstances change.

HONESTY IN SCRIPTURE

Hundreds of verses in the Bible communicate God's desire for us to be completely honest. For instance, Proverbs 20:23 says, *"The Lord loathes all cheating and dishonesty"* (TLB). And Proverbs 12:22 states, *"Lying lips are an abomination to the Lord."* And in Proverbs 6:16-17 we read, *"The Lord hates . . . a lying tongue."*

Study the following comparison between what the Scriptures teach and what our society practices concerning honesty.

THE GOD OF TRUTH

Truthfulness is one of God's attributes. He is repeatedly identified as the God of truth. *"I am . . . the truth"* (John 14:6). And He commands us to reflect His honest and holy character: *"Be holy yourselves also in all your behavior; because it is written, 'You shall be holy, for I am holy'"* (1 Peter 1:15-16).

In contrast to God's nature, John 8:44 describes the devil's character: *"He [the devil] was a murderer from the beginning, and does not stand in the truth because there is no truth in him.*

ISSUE	SCRIPTURE	SOCIETY
Standard of honesty:	Complete honesty	Changes with circumstances
God's concern about honesty:	He requires it	There is no God or He looks the other way
The decision to be honest or dishonest is based upon:	Faith in the invisible, living God	Only facts that can be seen
Question usually asked when deciding whether or not to be honest:	Will it please God?	Will I get away with it?

Whenever he speaks a lie, he speaks from his own nature, for he is a liar and the father of lies." The Lord wants us to conform to His honest character rather than to the dishonest nature of the devil.

ABSOLUTE HONESTY

God wants us to be completely honest for the following reasons.

1. We cannot practice dishonesty and love God.

Two of the Ten Commandments address honesty. *"You shall not steal. You shall not bear false witness against your neighbor"* (Exodus 20:15-16). And Jesus told us, *"If you love Me, you will keep My commandments"* (John 14:15).

We cannot disobey by practicing dishonesty and still love God. When being dishonest, we behave as if the living God doesn't even exist! We believe that He is unable to provide exactly what we need even though He has promised to do so (Matthew 6:33). We take the situation into our own hands and do it our own dishonest way. We are also acting as if God is incapable of discovering our dishonesty and powerless to discipline us. If we really believe God will discipline us, we will not consider acting dishonestly.

Honest behavior is an issue of faith. An honest decision may look foolish in light of what we can see, but the godly person knows Jesus Christ is alive even though invisible. Every honest decision strengthens our faith and helps us grow into a closer relationship with Christ. When we choose to be dishonest, we are denying our Lord. It is impossible to love God with all of our heart, soul, and mind if, at the same time, we are dishonest and act as if He does not exist. Scripture declares that the dishonest actually hate God. *"He who walks in his uprightness fears the Lord, but he who is crooked in his ways despises Him"* (Proverbs 14:2).

Wow! Before learning God's view of honesty, I had no clue He felt so strongly about it. I was often dishonest in my financial dealings. However, once I began breaking my dishonest habits, I realized that God's primary interest in our honesty is so that we can experience a closer relationship with Him.

2. We cannot practice dishonesty and love our neighbor.

God requires honesty because dishonest behavior also violates the second commandment, *"You shall love your neighbor as yourself"* (Mark 12:31). Romans 13:9-10 reads, *"If you love your neighbor as much as you love yourself you will not want to harm or cheat him, or kill him or steal from him. . . . Love does no wrong to anyone"* (TLB).

When we act dishonestly, we are stealing from another person. We may rationalize that it is a business or the government or an insurance company that is suffering loss. Yet, if we look at the bottom line, it is the business owners or fellow taxpayers or policy holders from whom we are stealing. It is just as if we took the money from their wallets. Dishonesty always injures people. The victim is always a person.

HONESTY ENABLES US TO DEMONSTRATE THE REALITY OF JESUS CHRIST.

3. Credibility for Evangelism

Honesty enables us to demonstrate the reality of Jesus Christ to those who do not yet know Him.

I will never forget the first time I told a neighbor how he could come to know Christ as his personal Savior. He angrily responded, "Well, I know a man who always goes to church and talks a lot about Jesus, but watch out if you ever get in a business deal with him! He'd cheat his own grandmother! If that's what it means to be a Christian, I don't want any part of it!"

Our actions speak louder than our words. *"Prove yourselves to be blameless and innocent, children of God above reproach in the midst of a crooked and perverse generation, among whom you appear as lights in the world"* (Philippians 2:15).

We can influence people for Jesus Christ by handling our money honestly. Robert Newsom had been trying to sell a car for months when someone finally made an acceptable offer. At the last moment, however, the buyer said, "I have one condition— you don't report this sale so I won't have to pay state sales tax."

Although he was tempted, Robert responded, "I'm sorry, I can't do that because Jesus Christ is my Lord." Robert later said, "You should have seen that guy's reaction. He almost went into shock! Then an interesting thing happened. His attitude completely changed. Not only did he buy the car, but he eagerly joined my wife and me at our dinner table. Rarely have I seen anyone as open to the truth about knowing Jesus Christ in a personal way."

Because Robert acted honestly, even though it was going to cost him money ("Prove yourselves to be blameless and innocent, children of God above reproach"), he demonstrated to this person ("a crooked and perverse generation") the reality of a personal faith in Jesus Christ ("appear as lights in the world").

HeyHoward@Crown.org

Q: *Is is permissible to reduce my taxes by using legal tax deductions?*

A: Yes! Absolutely! You should use legal tax deductions and pay whatever is due after your deductions.

4. Confirms God's Direction

Proverbs 4:24-26 reads, *"Put away from you a deceitful mouth and put devious speech far from you. Let your eyes look directly ahead and let your gaze be fixed straight in front of you. Watch the path of your feet and all your ways will be established."* What a tremendous principle. As you are completely honest, "all your ways will be established." Choosing to walk the narrow path of honesty eliminates the many possible avenues of dishonesty.

"If only I'd understood that," Raymond said. "Donna and I wanted that house so much. It was our dream home. But we had too much debt to qualify for the mortgage. The only way for us to buy it was to hide some of our debts from the bank.

"It was the worst decision of our lives. Almost immediately we were unable to meet the mortgage payment and pay our other debts too. The pressure built and was more than Donna could stand. Our dream house ended up being a family nightmare. I not only lost the house but nearly lost my wife."

Had Raymond and Donna been honest, the bank would not have approved the loan, and they would have been unable to purchase that particular home. Had they prayed and waited, God might have brought something more affordable, thus avoiding the pressure that almost ended their marriage. Honesty helps confirm God's direction.

5. Even Small Acts of Dishonesty Are Harmful

God requires us to be completely honest because even the smallest act of dishonesty is sin and interrupts our fellowship with God. The smallest "white lie" hardens our hearts, making our consciences increasingly insensitive to sin and deafening our ears to God's voice. This single cancer cell of small dishonesty multiplies and spreads to greater dishonesty. *"Whoever is dishonest with very little will also be dishonest with much"* (Luke 16:10, NIV).

An event in Abraham's life challenges us to be honest in small matters. The king of Sodom offered him all the goods he had recovered when he had rescued the people of Sodom. But Abraham responded, *"I have sworn to the Lord God Most High, possessor of heaven and earth, that I will not take a thread or a sandal thong or anything that is yours"* (Genesis 14:22-23).

Just as Abraham was unwilling to take so much as a thread, we challenge you to make a similar commitment. Decide not to steal a stamp or a photocopy or a paper clip or a long-distance telephone call or a penny from your employer, the government, or anyone else. The people of God must be honest in even the smallest matters.

To love God and our neighbors, to evangelize effectively, to confirm God's direction, and to develop a heart sensitive to God—is there any wonder that our Lord knows it is best for us to be completely honest?

ESCAPING THE TEMPTATION OF DISHONESTY

A friend was teaching these principles in a secular school when a young man raised his hand and said, "I think we all would like to be the person you're talking about, but I know in my heart that if the right opportunity comes along, I'm going to be dishonest." I think he is correct. Apart from living our lives yielded to the Holy Spirit, all of us will be dishonest.

> *"Live by the Spirit, and you will not gratify the desires of the sinful nature. For the sinful nature desires what is contrary to the Spirit, and the Spirit what is contrary to the sinful nature"* (Galatians 5:16-17, NIV).

"LIVE BY THE SPIRIT, AND YOU WILL NOT GRATIFY THE DESIRES OF THE SINFUL NATURE."

The character of our human nature is to act dishonestly. *"Out of men's hearts, come evil thoughts . . . theft . . . deceit"* (Mark 7:21-22, NIV). The desire of the Spirit is for us to be honest. The absolutely honest life is supernatural. We need to submit ourselves entirely to Jesus Christ as Lord and allow Him to live His life through us. There is no other way.

We heartily recommend a short book by Andrew Murray titled *Humility*. It is an excellent study for yielding fully to Christ.

The following principles will help you develop the habit of honesty.

1. Practice the Golden Rule.

"Do not merely look out for your own personal interests, but also for the interests of others" (Philippians 2:4). This verse is better translated, "look intently" after the interests of others. God used this passage to point out Warren's lack of concern for others just when he was about to purchase some land, taking advantage of a seller who knew nothing of its value. Warren secretly congratulated himself because he knew the purchase price he had offered was very low. Not once had he considered what would be fair to the seller. He had concentrated solely on acquiring the property at the lowest possible price.

Warren reexamined the transaction in the light of "looking intently" after the seller's interests as well as his own. After an intense inner struggle, he concluded that he should pay more for the property to reflect its true value. Practicing the Golden Rule is sometimes costly, but its reward is a clear conscience before God and other people.

2. Maintain a healthy fear of the Lord.

When we talk of a "healthy fear" of the Lord, we are not implying that God is a big bully just waiting for the opportunity to punish us. Rather, He is a loving Father who, out of infinite love, disciplines His children for their benefit. *"He disciplines us for our good, so that we may share His holiness"* (Hebrews 12:10).

One of the methods God uses to motivate honesty in us is this "healthy fear." Proverbs 16:6 says, *"By the fear of the Lord one keeps away from evil."* Hebrews 12:11 warns us: *"All discipline for the moment seems not to be joyful, but sorrowful."* Discipline hurts! Given the choice, we should obey His Word rather than make a deliberate decision that will prompt our loving Father to discipline us.

We believe our heavenly Father will not allow us to keep anything we have acquired dishonestly. Proverbs 13:11 reads, *"Wealth obtained by fraud dwindles."*

A friend purchased four azalea plants, but the checkout clerk had only charged her for one. She knew it, but she left the store without paying for the other three. She told me it was miraculous how quickly three of those plants died!

Think about this for a moment: If you are a parent and one of your children steals something, do you allow the child to keep it? Of course not, because keeping it would damage the child's character. Not only do you insist on its return, but you usually want the child to experience enough discomfort to produce a lasting impression. For instance, you might have the child confess the theft to the store manager. When our heavenly Father lovingly disciplines us, He usually does it in a way we will not forget.

3. Stay away from dishonest people.

Scripture teaches that we are deeply influenced by those around us, either for good or for evil. David recognized this and said, *"My eyes shall be upon the faithful of the land, that they may dwell with me; he who walks in a blameless way is the one who will minister to me. He who practices deceit shall not dwell within my house; he who speaks falsehood shall not maintain his position before me"* (Psalm 101:6-7). Paul wrote, *"Do not be deceived: 'Bad company corrupts good morals'"* (1 Corinthians 15:33). Solomon was even stronger: *"He who is a partner with a thief hates his own life"* (Proverbs 29:24).

Obviously, we cannot isolate ourselves from every dishonest person. In fact, we are to be "salt and light" in the world (Matthew 5:13-16). We should, however, be very cautious when choosing our close friends or considering a business relationship with another.

If I observe a person who is dishonest in dealing with the government or in a small matter, I know this person will be dishonest in greater matters and probably in dealing with me. In our opinion, it is impossible for people to be selectively honest. Either they have made the commitment to be completely honest or their dishonesty will become more prevalent. It is much easier to remain absolutely honest if you are surrounded by others with the same conviction.

4. Give generously.

We can help escape the temptation of acting dishonestly by giving generously to those in need. *"He who steals must steal no longer; but rather he must labor, performing with his own hands what is good, so that he will have something to share with one who has need"* (Ephesians 4:28).

Giving draws us closer to Christ and reduces our incentive to steal. After all, if we are going to give something away, there's no reason to steal it!

WHAT TO DO WHEN WE HAVE BEEN DISHONEST

Unfortunately, we sometimes slip and act dishonestly. Once we recognize it, we need to do the following.

1. Restore our fellowship with God.

Anytime we sin, we break fellowship with God and need to restore it. First John 1:9 tells us how: *"If we confess our sins, He is faithful and righteous to forgive us our sins and to cleanse us from all unrighteousness."* We must agree with God that our dishonesty was sin and then thankfully accept His gracious forgiveness so we can again enjoy His fellowship. Remember, God loves us. He is kind and merciful. God is ready to forgive our dishonesty when we turn from it.

2. Restore our fellowship with the harmed person.

After our fellowship with God has been restored, we need to confess our dishonesty to the person we offended. *"Confess your sins to one another"* (James 5:16).

Ouch! This hurts. Only a handful of people have confessed wronging me. Interestingly, these people have become some of my closest friends—in part because of my respect for them. They so desired an honest relationship that they were willing to expose their sins.

Confessing has been very hard for me. My first experience came several years ago when I went to someone I had wronged and confessed my sin—not that I hadn't had plenty of opportunities before! In the past, however, my pride had stood in the way. Afterward I sensed a great freedom in our relationship. I also discovered that, because it is a painfully humbling experience, confession helps break the habit of dishonesty.

Failing to confess and restore fellowship may result in a lack of financial prosperity. *"He who conceals his transgressions will not prosper, but he who confesses and forsakes them will find compassion"* (Proverbs 28:13).

3. Restore dishonestly acquired property.

If we have acquired anything dishonestly, we must return it to its rightful owner. *"Then it shall be, when he sins and becomes guilty, that he shall restore what he took by robbery . . . or anything about which he swore falsely; he shall make restitution for it in full and add to it one-fifth more. He shall give it to the one to whom it belongs"* (Leviticus 6:4-5).

Restitution is a tangible expression of repentance and an effort to correct a wrong. Zaccheus is a good example. He promised Jesus, *"If I have defrauded anyone of anything, I will give back four times as much"* (Luke 19:8).

If it's not possible for restitution to be made, then the property should be given to God. Numbers 5:8 teaches, *"If the man has no relative to whom restitution may be made for the wrong, the restitution which is made for the wrong must go to the Lord."*

RESTITUTION IS A TANGIBLE EXPRESSION OF REPENTANCE.

HONESTY REQUIRED FOR LEADERS

God is especially concerned with the honesty of leaders.

Influence of Leaders

Leaders influence those who follow them. The owner of a trucking business began wearing cowboy boots to work. Within six months, all the men in his office were in boots. He suddenly changed to traditional business shoes, and six months later all the men were wearing business shoes.

In a similar way, a dishonest leader produces dishonest followers. *"If a ruler pays attention to falsehood, all his ministers become wicked"* (Proverbs 29:12). Leaders of a business, church, or home must set the example of honesty in their personal life before those under their authority can be expected to do the same.

The president of a large international construction company was asked why her company did not work in countries where bribes were common. She responded, "We never build in those countries because we can't afford to. If my employees know we are acting dishonestly, they will eventually become thieves. Their dishonesty will ultimately cost us more than we could ever earn on a project."

During an effort to reduce expenses, a company discovered the employees were making frequent personal long-distance telephone calls at the office and charging them to the company. The company president had unwittingly fueled this problem. He had reasoned that because he placed approximately the same number of company long-distance calls on his home phone as personal long-distance calls on the company phone, a detailed accounting was unnecessary. His employees, however, knew only of his calls at work. They concluded that if this practice was acceptable for the boss, it was acceptable for all. Leaders should *"abstain from all appearance of evil"* (1 Thessalonians 5:22, KJV) because their actions influence others.

Selection of Leaders

Dishonesty should disqualify a person from leadership. Listen to the counsel of Jethro, Moses' father-in-law.

"You shall select out of all the people able men who fear God, men of truth, those who hate dishonest gain; and you shall place these . . . as leaders of thousands, of hundreds, of fifties and of tens" (Exodus 18:21).

Two of the four criteria for leadership selection dealt with honesty: "men of truth, those who hate dishonest gain." We believe God wants us to continue to select leaders based on these same character qualities.

Preservation of Leaders

Not only are leaders selected in part by honest behavior, but a leader retains this position by acting honestly. *"A leader . . . who hates unjust gain will prolong his days"* (Proverbs 28:16). We have all witnessed leaders in business or government who have been removed because of personal corruption.

How can a leader maintain the standard of absolute honesty? By becoming accountable to others. It is necessary to establish a system of checks and balances that do not usurp the leader's authority but provide a structure to ensure accountability.

BRIBES

A bribe is defined as anything given to influence a person to do something illegal or wrong. The taking of bribes is clearly prohibited in Scripture: *"You shall not take a bribe, for a bribe blinds the clear-sighted and subverts the cause of the just"* (Exodus 23:8). Bribes frequently come packaged as "gifts" or "referral fees." Evaluate any such offer to confirm that it is not a bribe in disguise.

BLESSINGS AND CURSES

Listed below are some of the blessings God has promised for the honest and some of the curses reserved for the dishonest. Read these slowly and prayerfully, asking God to use His Word to motivate you to a life of honesty.

Blessings for the honest:

- Blessing of a more intimate relationship with the Lord. *"For the crooked man is an abomination to the Lord; but He is intimate with the upright"* (Proverbs 3:32).

- Blessings on the family. *"A righteous man who walks in his integrity—how blessed are his sons after him"* (Proverbs 20:7).

- Blessings of life. *"Truthful lips will be established forever, but a lying tongue is only for a moment"* (Proverbs 12:19).

- Blessings of prosperity. *"Much wealth is in the house of the righteous, but trouble is in the income of the wicked"* (Proverbs 15:6).

Curses reserved for the dishonest:

- Curse of alienation from God. *"For the crooked man is an abomination to the Lord"* (Proverbs 3:32).

- Curse on the family. *"He who profits illicitly troubles his own house, but he who hates bribes will live"* (Proverbs 15:27).

- Curse of death. *"The getting of treasures by a lying tongue is a fleeting vapor, the pursuit of death"* (Proverbs 21:6).

- Curse of poverty. *"Wealth obtained by fraud dwindles"* (Proverbs 13:11).

Startling Statistics

- *There are 23 million shoplifters in America who steal more than $10 billion of merchandise a year. About 75 percent of shoplifters are adults.*

MY NOTES

GIVING

Giving is blessed.

Scripture to Memorize

"Remember the words of the Lord Jesus, that He Himself said, 'It is more blessed to give than to receive'" (Acts 20:35).

Practical Application

Complete the Beginning Your Spending Plan, the Spending Plan Analysis, and review Destination 3 on the _Crown Money Map._™

Day One - Let's Review Honesty

Read the Honesty Notes on pages 64-71 and answer:

1. How does the example of Abraham (Abram) in Genesis 14:21-23 challenge you to be honest?

2. Ask God to reveal any areas of dishonesty in your life. How do you propose to deal with these areas?

GIVING

Day Two

Read Matthew 23:23; 1 Corinthians 13:3; and 2 Corinthians 9:7.

1. What do each of these passages communicate about the importance of the proper attitude in giving?

   Matthew 23:23 –

   1 Corinthians 13:3 –

   2 Corinthians 9:7 –

2. How do you think a person can develop the proper attitude in giving?

3. How would you describe your attitude in giving?

Day Three

Read Acts 20:35.

1. How does this principle from God's economy differ from the way most people view giving?

Read Proverbs 11:24-25; Matthew 6:20; Luke 12:34; and 1 Timothy 6:18-19.

2. List the benefits for the giver that are found in each of the following passages.

Proverbs 11:24-25 –

Matthew 6:20 –

Luke 12:34 –

1 Timothy 6:18-19 –

Day Four

Read Malachi 3:8-10.

1. How did God view the failure to tithe (give 10 percent)?

Read 2 Corinthians 8:1-5.

2. Identify three principles from this passage that should influence how much you give.

Prayerfully (with your spouse if you are married) seek the Lord's guidance to determine how much you should give. You will not be asked to disclose the amount.

Day Five

Read Numbers 18:8-10, 24; Galatians 6:6; and 1 Timothy 5:17-18.

1. What do these verses tell you about financially supporting your church and those who teach the Scriptures?

Numbers 18:8-10, 24 –

Galatians 6:6 –

1 Timothy 5:17-18 –

Day Six

Read Isaiah 58:6-11 and Ezekiel 16:49.

1. What do these verses say about giving to the poor?

Isaiah 58:6-11 –

Ezekiel 16:49 –

Read Matthew 25:35-45.

2. How does Jesus Christ identify with the needy?

Read Galatians 2:9-10.

3. What does this verse communicate to you about giving to the poor?

4. Are you currently giving to the needy? If not, what is hindering you?

Follow-up

☑ Please write your prayer requests in your prayer log before coming to the meeting.

☑ I will take the following action as a result of this week's study:

Few areas of the Christian life can be more misunderstood and frustrating than that of giving. For several years after I met Christ, I did my best to avoid giving. On those occasions when I felt obligated to give in order to appear spiritual, I did so, but my heart wasn't in it.

My whole perspective changed after learning what the Bible actually teaches. Suddenly I wanted to give, but then I was frustrated by another problem: an unlimited number of needs versus my limited resources. How should I decide where to give? My church, the hungry and poor, campus and prison ministries, missionary efforts, radio and television programs, and many other vital ministries needed financial support.

Intense competition for resources makes these decisions even more difficult. It seems as if my mailbox is constantly full of appeals. I react to these requests with mixed emotions: compassion, gratitude, guilt, and even cynicism. I feel deep compassion and almost despair when confronted with those facing starvation of body or spirit. I am grateful for the people whose life purpose is to meet those needs. I feel guilty that perhaps we are not giving enough. Sometimes I feel cynical about being solicited and perhaps manipulated by people whose goals may be worthwhile but whose methods are questionable.

We will examine four elements of giving: attitudes, advantages, amount, and approach.

ATTITUDES IN GIVING

ABOVE ALL ELSE, GIVING DIRECTS OUR HEART TO CHRIST.

God evaluates our actions on the basis of our attitudes. John 3:16 reveals His attitude toward giving: *"For God so loved the world, that He gave His only begotten Son."* Note the sequence. Because God loved, He gave. Because God is love, He is also a giver. He set the example of giving motivated by love.

An attitude of love in giving is crucial: *"If I give all my possessions to feed the poor . . . but do not have love, it profits me nothing"* (1 Corinthians 13:3). What could be more commendable than giving everything to the poor? However, giving without an attitude of love provides no benefit to the giver.

In God's economy, the attitude is more important than the amount. Jesus emphasized this in Matthew 23:23: *"Woe to you, teachers of the law and Pharisees, you hypocrites! You give a tenth of your spices—mint, dill and cummin. But you have neglected the more important matters of the law—justice, mercy and faithfulness. You should have practiced the latter without neglecting the former"* (NIV). The Pharisees had been careful to give the correct amount, but Christ rebuked them because of their attitude. He looks past the amount of the gift to the heart of the giver.

We can consistently give with love when we recognize that we are giving to God Himself. We see an example of this in Numbers 18:24: *"The tithe of the sons of Israel . . . they offer as an offering **to the Lord**"* [emphasis mine]. If giving is merely to a church, a ministry, or a needy person, it is only charity. But giving to God is always an act of worship, expressing love and gratitude to our Creator, our Savior, and our faithful Provider. Whenever we put something in the offering plate, we should remind ourselves that our gift goes to God Himself.

In addition to giving with love, we are to give cheerfully. *"Each one must do just as he has purposed in his heart, not grudgingly or under compulsion, for God loves a cheerful giver"* (2 Corinthians 9:7). The original Greek word for cheerful is *hilarios*, which is translated into the English word *hilarious*. We are to be joyful givers.

When was the last time you saw hilarity when the offering plate passed? The atmosphere more often reminds us of a patient in the dentist chair awaiting a painful extraction. So, how do we develop this hilarity in our giving? Consider the early churches of Macedonia.

"We want you to know about the grace that God has given the Macedonian churches. Out of the most severe trial, their overflowing joy and their extreme poverty welled up in rich generosity" (2 Corinthians 8:1-2, NIV).

How did the Macedonians, who were in terrible circumstances, "severe trial" and "extreme poverty," still manage to give with "overflowing joy"? The answer is in verse 5: *"They gave themselves first to the Lord and then to us in keeping with God's will."* The key to cheerful giving is to yield ourselves to Christ and ask Him to direct how much He wants us to give. That places us in a position to experience the advantages of giving with the proper attitude.

Stop and examine yourself. What is your attitude toward giving?

ADVANTAGES OF GIVING

Gifts obviously benefit the recipient. The church continues its ministry, the hungry are fed, the naked are clothed, and missionaries are sent. But in God's economy, gifts given with the proper attitude benefit the giver more than the receiver. *"Remember the words of the Lord Jesus, that He Himself said, 'It is more blessed to give than to receive'"* (Acts 20:35). As we examine Scripture, we find that the giver benefits in four significant areas.

1. Increase in Intimacy

Above all else, giving directs our hearts to Christ. Matthew 6:21 tells us, *"For where your treasure is, there your heart will be also."* This is why it is necessary to give each gift to the person of Jesus Christ: It draws our heart to Him.

Do you remember the faithful steward in the parable of the talents? His reward— *"enter into the joy of your Master"* (Matthew 25:21). Giving is one of your responsibilities as a steward; and the more faithful you are in fulfilling your responsibilities, the more you can enter into the joy of knowing Christ intimately. Nothing in life compares with that.

2. Increase in Character

Our heavenly Father wants us—His children—to conform to the image of His Son. The character of Christ is that of an unselfish giver. Unfortunately, humans are selfish by nature. One essential way we become conformed to Christ is by regular giving.

Someone once said, "Giving is not God's way of raising money; it is God's way of raising people into the likeness of His Son."

3. Increase in Heaven

Matthew 6:20 reads, *"Store up for yourselves treasures in heaven, where neither moth nor rust destroys, and where thieves do not break in or steal."* God tells us that heaven has its own "First National Bank," where we can invest for eternity.

Paul wrote, *"Not that I seek the gift itself, but I seek for the profit which increases to your account"* (Philippians 4:17). Each of us has an account in heaven that we will be able to enjoy for eternity. And although it is true that we "can't take it with us when we die," Scripture teaches that we can make deposits to our heavenly account before we die.

4. Increase on Earth

Many people have a hard time believing that giving results in material blessings flowing back to the giver; however, study the following passages.

Proverbs 11:24-25 says, *"There is one who scatters, and yet increases all the more, and there is one who withholds what is justly due, and yet it results only in want. The generous man will be prosperous, and he who waters will himself be watered."*

Examine 2 Corinthians 9:6-11. *"He who sows sparingly will also reap sparingly, and he who sows bountifully will also reap bountifully. . . . God is able to make all grace abound to you, so that always having all sufficiency in everything, you may have an abundance for every good deed. . . . Now He who supplies seed to the sower and bread for food will supply and multiply your seed for sowing and increase the harvest of your righteousness; you will be enriched in everything for all liberality."*

These verses clearly teach that giving results in a material increase: "will also reap bountifully . . . always having all sufficiency in everything . . . may have an abundance . . . will supply and multiply your seed . . . you will be enriched in everything."

But note carefully why God returns a material increase: "Always having all sufficiency in everything, you may have an abundance for every good deed . . . will supply and multiply your seed for sowing . . . you will be enriched in everything for all liberality." As shown in the diagram below, the Lord produces an increase so that we may give more and have our needs met at the same time.

Give

Material Increase

Needs Met

STUDY THE CYCLE OF GIVING.

One reason God reveals that we can anticipate a material increase is because He wants us to recognize that He is behind it. God has chosen to be invisible, but He wants us to experience His reality.

When we give, we should do so with a sense of anticipating a material increase from God even though we do not know how or when He may choose to provide it. Our experience has shown Him to be very creative! Remember, givers experience the advantages of giving only when they give cheerfully and with love—not when the motive is just to get.

AMOUNT TO GIVE

Let's survey what the Bible says about how much to give. Before the Old Testament Law, there were two instances of giving a known amount. In Genesis 14:20, Abraham (Abram) gave 10 percent—a tithe—after the rescue of his nephew Lot. And in Genesis 28:22, Jacob promised to give God a tenth of all his possessions if God brought him safely through his journey.

With the Law came the requirement of the tithe. The Lord condemns the children of Israel in Malachi 3:8-9 for not tithing properly: *"Will a man rob God? Yet you are robbing Me! But you say, 'How have we robbed You?' In tithes and offerings. You are cursed with a curse, for you are robbing Me, the whole nation of you!"*

In addition to the tithe, there were various offerings. God also made special provisions for the poor. Every seven years all debts were forgiven; every 50 years the land was returned to the original land-owning families. Special harvesting rules allowed the poor to glean behind the harvesters.

God made another significant provision for the poor in Deuteronomy 15:7-8: *"If there is a poor man with you, one of your brothers, in any of your towns in your land which the Lord your God is giving you, you shall not harden your heart, nor close your hand from your poor brother; but you shall freely open your hand to him, and shall generously lend him sufficient for his need in whatever he lacks."* Even under the law, the extent of one's giving was not to be limited by a fixed percentage but was to be adjusted by surrounding needs.

The New Testament teaches that we are to give in proportion to the material blessing we receive. It also commends sacrificial giving.

What I like about the tithe is that it is systematic, and the amount of the gift is easy to compute. The danger of the tithe is that it can be treated as simply another bill to be paid; this attitude does not place us in a position to receive the blessings God has for us when we give. Another potential danger of tithing is the assumption that once we have tithed we have fulfilled all of our obligations to give. For many Christians, the tithe should be the beginning of their giving, not the limit.

How much should you give? To answer this question, first give yourself to God. Submit yourself to Him. Earnestly seek His will for you concerning giving. Ask Him to help you obey Christ's leading. We are convinced that we should tithe as a minimum and then give over and above the tithe as God prospers or directs us.

APPROACH TO GIVING

During Paul's third missionary journey, one of his priorities was to take up a collection for the suffering believers in Jerusalem. We draw several practical applications from his instructions concerning this collection. *"On the first day of every week each one of you is to put aside and save, as he may prosper, so that no collections be made when I come"* (1 Corinthians 16:2).

1. Giving should be periodic.

"On the first day of every week." God understands that we need to give frequently. Giving only once a year is a mistake. We need to give regularly to be drawn consistently to Christ.

2. Giving should be personal.

"Each one of you is to." It is the responsibility of every child of God, whether young or old, rich or poor, to give. The advantages of giving are intended for each person, and each one must participate to enjoy them.

3. Giving should be out of a private deposit.

"Put aside and save." If you experience difficulty in monitoring the money you have decided to give, consider opening a separate account or setting aside a special "cookie jar" into which you deposit the money you intend to give. Then, as needs are brought to your attention, the money is ready to meet those needs.

4. Giving should be a priority.

"Honor the Lord from your wealth and from the first of all your produce" (Proverbs 3:9). As soon as we receive any income, we should set aside the amount we are going to give. This habit helps us to put Christ first in all we do and defeats the temptation to spend what we have decided to give.

5. Giving should be premeditated.

"Each one must do just as he has purposed in his heart" (2 Corinthians 9:7). We should give prayerfully, exercising the same care in selecting where we give as we do when deciding where to invest.

DO NOT GIVE TO IMPRESS PEOPLE.

6. Giving should be without pride.

To experience any of God's benefits, do not give to impress people. Matthew 6:1-4 says, "Be careful not to do your 'acts of righteousness' before men, to be seen by them. If you do, you will have no reward from your Father in heaven. So when you give to the needy, do not announce it with trumpets, as the hypocrites do in the synagogues and on the streets, to be honored by men. . . . They have received their reward in full. But when you give to the needy, do not let your left hand know what your right hand is doing, so that your giving may be in secret. Then your Father, who sees what is done in secret, will reward you" (NIV).

PLACES FOR GIVING

In the Bible we are instructed to give to three areas: the local church, ministries, and the poor and needy.

1. Giving to the Local Church and Christian Ministries

Throughout its pages, the Bible focuses on funding the ministry. The Old Testament priesthood received specific support: "To the sons of Levi, behold, I have given all the tithe in Israel . . . in return for their service which they perform" (Numbers 18:21). And New Testament teaching on ministerial support is just as strong. Unfortunately, some have wrongly taught poverty for Christian workers, influencing many to believe that everyone in Christian ministry should be poor. That position is not scriptural.

"Pastors who do their work well should be paid well and should be highly appreciated, especially those who work hard at both preaching and teaching" (1 Timothy 5:17, TLB).

God never intended His servants to exist at the level of bare subsistence, but many Christian workers have been distracted from their ministry by inadequate support. As someone has said, "The poor and starving pastor should exist only among poor and starving people."

People ask us if we give only through our church. In our case, the answer is "no." However, giving to the local church should be a priority. We give a minimum of 10 percent of our regular income through our church as a tangible expression of our commitment to it. But we also give to others who directly impact us. *"The one who is taught the word is to share all good things with the one who teaches"* (Galatians 6:6).

2. Giving to the Poor

Matthew 25:34-45 teaches one of the most exciting and yet sobering truths in Scripture. Read this passage carefully.

"The King will say . . . 'For I was hungry and you gave Me something to eat; I was thirsty, and you gave Me something to drink.' . . . Then the righteous will answer Him, 'Lord, when did we see You hungry, and feed You, or thirsty, and give You something to drink?' . . . The King will answer and say to them . . . 'To the extent that you did it to one of these brothers of Mine, even the least of them, you did it to Me.' Then He will also say to those on His left, 'Depart from Me, accursed ones, into the eternal fire . . . for I was hungry, and you gave Me nothing to eat; I was thirsty, and you gave Me nothing to drink. . . . To the extent that you did not do it to one of the least of these, you did not do it to Me.'"

In a mysterious way we cannot fully understand, Jesus, the Creator of all things, personally identifies Himself with the poor. When we share with the needy, we are actually sharing with Jesus Himself. If that truth is staggering, then this is terrifying: When we do not give to the needy, we leave Christ Himself hungry and thirsty.

During Christ's earthly ministry, He consistently gave to the poor. When Jesus told Judas to go and carry out the betrayal during the Last Supper, *"no one of those reclining at the table knew for what purpose He had said this to him. For some were supposing, because Judas had the money box, that Jesus was saying to him, 'Buy things we have need of for the feast'; or else, that he should give something to the poor"* (John 13:28-29).

Giving to the needy was such a consistent part of Jesus' life that the disciples assumed He was sending Judas either to buy needed food or to give to the poor; no other alternative entered their minds.

After Paul met with the disciples to announce his ministry to the Gentiles, he said, *"They [the disciples] only asked us to remember the poor—the very thing I also was eager to do"* (Galatians 2:10). Think of all the issues the disciples could have discussed with Paul. But the only request they made was to remember the poor. Now that should tell us something!

Three areas of our Christian life are affected by whether we give to the poor.

1. Prayer

A lack of giving to the poor could be a source of unanswered prayer. *"Is this not the fast which I choose . . . to divide your bread with the hungry and bring the homeless*

JESUS, THE CREATOR OF ALL THINGS, PERSONALLY IDENTIFIES HIMSELF WITH THE POOR.

poor into the house? . . . Then you will call and the Lord will answer" (Isaiah 58:6-9). "He who shuts his ear to the cry of the poor will also cry himself and not be answered" (Proverbs 21:13).

2. Provision

Our giving to the needy may determine our provision. "He who gives to the poor will never want, but he who shuts his eyes will have many curses" (Proverbs 28:27).

3. Knowing Jesus Christ intimately

Those who do not share with the poor do not know God as intimately as they could. "'He pled the cause of the afflicted and the needy; then it was well. Is that not what it means to know Me?' declares the Lord" (Jeremiah 22:16).

Giving to the poor has been discouraged, in part, because of government programs. We believe it is the church's job, not the government's, to meet the needs of the poor. The government often treats the needy impersonally. The church has the potential to be sensitive to their dignity. We can also develop one-on-one relationships to meet their immediate physical needs and then focus on their longer-term physical and spiritual needs. Mother Teresa is one of the best examples in our time of serving the poor in a loving, compassionate way.

If you don't already know some needy people, please consider asking the Lord to bring one into your life. You can do so by praying this prayer: "Father God, by Your grace, create in me the desire to share with the needy. Bring a poor person into my life so that I might learn what it really means to give." This will be a significant step in maturing your relationship with Christ.

May we echo Job's statement: "I delivered the poor who cried for help, and the orphan who had no helper. . . . I made the widow's heart sing for joy. . . . I was eyes to the blind and feet to the lame. I was a father to the needy, and I investigated the case which I did not know" (Job 29:12-16).

SECULAR CHARITIES

Numerous secular charities (schools, fraternal orders, organizations that fight diseases) compete vigorously for our donations. Scripture does not address whether we should give to these charities. However, our family has decided not to make these organizations part of our regular giving. Our reason is that even though many people support secular charities, only those who know the Lord support the ministries of Christ. We do, however, occasionally give to secular charities when the solicitor is a friend we want to encourage or influence for Christ, or we sense God's prompting to give.

HeyHoward@Crown.org

Q: *I thought the Bible says that if I give generously, God is supposed to prosper me. Why hasn't this happened? I'm confused.*

A: It's important that you handle **all** your money God's way. Some people are generous, but suffer financially because they're dishonest or they don't work hard or they use credit to spend more than they can afford.

Q: *Should we tithe to our local church?*

A: In my opinion you should give at least 10 percent of your income to your church, and then give to other ministries and needs as God directs and provides.

"Whatever you do, do your work heartily, as for the Lord rather than for men. . . . It is the Lord Christ whom you serve" (Colossians 3:23-24).

WORK

Work diligently as unto the Lord.

HOMEWORK

Scripture to Memorize

"Whatever you do, do your work heartily, as for the Lord rather than for men. . . . It is the Lord Christ whom you serve" (Colossians 3:23-24).

Practical Application

Review the Spending Plan Hints, complete your Idea List, and review Tools for the Journey on the *Crown Money Map.*™

Note: Please give your leader the name of anyone who would be interested in becoming a student in a future group.

Day One - Let's Review Giving

Read the Giving Notes on pages 78-84 and answer:

1. From God's perspective it is important to give with the proper attitude. How will this impact your giving?

2. What truth about giving did you learn that proved especially helpful? In what way?

WORK

Day Two

Read Genesis 2:15.

1. Why is it important to recognize that the Lord created work before sin entered the world?

Read Genesis 3:17-19.

2. What was the consequence of sin on work?

Read Exodus 20:9 and 2 Thessalonians 3:10-12.

3. What do these passages say to you about work?

Exodus 20:9 –

2 Thessalonians 3:10-12 –

Day Three

Read Genesis 39:2-5; Exodus 35:30-35; Exodus 36:1-2; and Psalm 75:6-7.

1. What do these verses tell us about the Lord's involvement in our work?

Genesis 39:2-5 –

Exodus 35:30-35 –

Exodus 36:1-2 –

Psalm 75:6-7 –

2. How do these truths differ from the way most people view work?

3. How will this perspective impact your work?

Day Four

Read Ephesians 6:5-9; Colossians 3:22-25; and 1 Peter 2:18.

1. What responsibilities do the employee and employer have according to these verses?

   Employee responsibilities –

   Employer responsibilities –

2. For whom do you really work? How will this understanding change your work performance?

Day Five

Read Proverbs 6:6-11; Proverbs 18:9; and 2 Thessalonians 3:7-9.

1. What does God say about working hard?

   Proverbs 6:6-11 –

   Proverbs 18:9 –

   2 Thessalonians 3:7-9 –

2. Do you work hard? If not, describe what steps you will take to improve your work habits.

Read Exodus 34:21.

3. What does this verse communicate to you about rest?

4. Do you get enough rest?

5. How do you guard against working too much?

Day Six

Read Proverbs 31:10-28 and Titus 2:4-5.

1. What do these passages tell us about women working?

    Proverbs 31:10-28 –

    Titus 2:4-5 –

2. If you are a woman, how does this apply to your situation?

Read 2 Corinthians 6:14-18.

3. How does this concept of "yoking" or "being bound together" apply to partnerships in business and work?

4. Can you give some examples from the Bible of people who retired?

5. Do you think retirement, as it is practiced in our culture, is biblically acceptable? Why or why not?

Follow-up

☑ Please write your prayer requests in your prayer log before coming to the meeting.

☑ I will take the following action as a result of this week's study:

Over a lifetime, the average person spends 100,000 hours working. But, often with the job comes some degree of dissatisfaction. Perhaps no statistic demonstrates this more than job-change frequency. A survey found that the average man changes jobs every four and one-half years, and the average woman, every three years.

Boredom, lack of fulfillment, inadequate wages, and countless other pressures have contributed to this discontentment. Doctors, housewives, salespersons, blue-collar workers, managers, all—regardless of profession—have expressed similar frustrations. Understanding scriptural principles that relate to work will help you find satisfaction in your job. Implementing them will position you to increase your income.

GOD'S PERSPECTIVE OF WORK

Despite what many believe, work was initiated for our benefit in the sinless environment of the garden of Eden. Work is not a result of the curse! *"The Lord God took the man and put him into the garden of Eden to cultivate it and keep it"* (Genesis 2:15). The very first thing God did with Adam was to put him to work.

After the fall, work became more difficult. *"Cursed is the ground because of you; in toil you will eat of it all the days of your life. Both thorns and thistles it shall grow for you; and you will eat the plants of the field; by the sweat of your face you will eat bread"* (Genesis 3:17-19).

Work is so important that in Exodus 34:21 God gives this command: *"You shall work six days."* The Apostle Paul is just as direct: *"If anyone is not willing to work, then he is not to eat"* (2 Thessalonians 3:10). Examine the verse carefully. It says, *"If anyone is not willing to work."* It does not say, "If anyone cannot work." This principle does not apply to those who are physically or mentally unable to work; it is for those who are able but choose not to work.

A close friend has a brother in his mid-40s whose parents have always supported him. He has never had to face the responsibilities and hardships involved in a job. Consequently, his character has not been properly developed, leaving him hopelessly immature in many areas of his life.

ONE OF THE PRIMARY PURPOSES OF WORK IS TO DEVELOP CHARACTER.

One of the primary purposes of work is to develop character. While the carpenter is building a house, the house is also building the carpenter. The carpenter's skill, diligence, manual dexterity, and judgment are refined. A job is not merely a task designed to earn money; it's also intended to produce godly character in the life of the worker.

ALL HONEST PROFESSIONS ARE HONORABLE

Scripture gives dignity to all types of work, not elevating any honest profession above another. David was a shepherd and a king. Luke was a doctor. Lydia was a retailer of purple fabric. Daniel was a government worker. Paul was a tentmaker. Mary was a homemaker. And, finally, the Lord Jesus was a carpenter.

In God's economy, there is equal dignity in the labor of the automobile mechanic and the president of General Motors, in the labor of the pastor and a secretary serving the church.

GOD'S PART IN WORK

Scripture reveals three responsibilities the Lord has in our work.

1. God gives job skills.

Exodus 36:1 illustrates this truth: *"Every skillful person in whom the Lord has put skill and understanding to know how to perform all the work . . . shall perform."* God has given each of us unique aptitudes. People have a wide variety of abilities, manual skills, and intellectual capacities. It is not a matter of one person being better than another, merely that each has received different abilities.

2. God gives success.

The life of Joseph is a perfect example of God helping a person to succeed. *"The Lord was with Joseph, so he became a successful man. . . . His master saw that the Lord was with him and how the Lord caused all that he did to prosper"* (Genesis 39:2-3). Although we have certain responsibilities, it is ultimately God who gives success.

3. God controls promotion.

Psalm 75:6-7 says, *"For promotion and power come from nowhere on earth, but only from God"* (TLB). As much as it may surprise you, our bosses are not the ones who control whether we will be promoted. Many people leave God out of work, believing that they alone are responsible for their abilities and successes. One of the major reasons they experience stress and frustration in their jobs is because they don't understand God's part in work. Consider this question for a few minutes: If God gives you your abilities and controls success and promotion, how should this perspective affect your work?

OUR PART IN WORK

RECOGNIZING THAT WE WORK FOR THE LORD HAS PROFOUND IMPLICATIONS.

Did you know that in our work we actually serve God rather than people? *"Whatever you do, do your work heartily, as for the Lord rather than for men. . . . It is the Lord Christ whom you serve"* (Colossians 3:23-24). Recognizing that we work for God has profound implications. If you could see Jesus Christ as your boss, would you try to be more faithful in your job? The most important question you need to answer every day as you begin your work is this: "For whom do I work?" You work for Christ.

WORK HARD

"Whatever your hand finds to do, do it with all your might" (Ecclesiastes 9:10, NIV). *"The precious possession of a man is diligence"* (Proverbs 12:27). Scripture encourages hard work and diligence; laziness is condemned: *"He who is slack in his work is brother to him who destroys"* (Proverbs 18:9).

Paul's life was an example of hard work. *"With labor and hardship we kept working night and day so that we might not be a burden to any of you . . . in order to offer ourselves as a model for you, so that you might follow our example"* (2 Thessalonians 3:8-9).

Your work should never be at such a level that people will equate laziness with God. Nothing less than hard work and the pursuit of excellence pleases Him. He does not require us to be "superworkers" who never make mistakes, but He does expect us to do the best we possibly can.

BUT DO NOT OVERWORK!

Hard work, however, must be balanced by the other priorities of life. If your job demands so much of your time and energy that you neglect your relationship with Christ or your loved ones, then you are working too much. Determine whether the job itself is too demanding or whether your work habits need changing. If you tend to be a workaholic, be careful not to shortchange the other priorities of life.

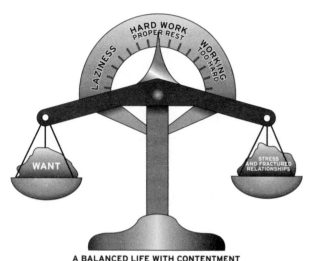

A BALANCED LIFE WITH CONTENTMENT

Exodus 34:21 reads, *"You shall work six days, but on the seventh day you shall rest; even during plowing time and harvest you shall rest."* We believe this Old Testament principle of resting one day out of seven has application today. This has been difficult for me, particularly during times of "plowing or harvesting," when a project deadline approaches or I am under financial pressure.

Rest can become an issue of faith. Is God able to make our six days of work more productive than seven? Yes! The Lord instituted weekly rest for our physical, mental, and spiritual health. Study this illustration to understand the balance God wants in our lives.

EMPLOYER'S RESPONSIBILITIES

Godly employers perform a balancing act. They are to love, serve, and encourage employees while leading them and holding them accountable for the completion of their assigned tasks. Let's examine several principles that should govern an employer's conduct.

1. Serve your employees.

The basis for biblical leadership is servanthood: *"Whoever wishes to become great among you shall be your servant"* (Matthew 20:26). Employers often concentrate on producing a profit at the expense of their personnel. However, the Bible directs them to balance efforts to make a profit with an unselfish concern for employees, treating them with fairness and dignity. *"Masters [employers], grant to your slaves [employees] justice and fairness, knowing that you too have a Master in heaven"* (Colossians 4:1).

Employers should attempt to be creative as they serve their employees. For example, investing time and money to educate and upgrade their employees' job skills will help employees grow in value and earning power.

2. Be a good communicator.

The Genesis account of building the tower of Babel supports the importance of good communication. At that time, everyone spoke the same language and adopted a common goal. The Lord makes this remarkable observation, *"If as one people speaking the same language they have begun to do this, then nothing they plan to do will be impossible for them"* (Genesis 11:6, NIV).

When people have good communication and pursue a common goal, then "nothing they plan to do will be impossible for them"—as long as it's within the will of God. Since building the tower was not what He wanted, He stopped construction. And how did God do it? He disrupted their ability to communicate, which was the foundation for successfully completing the tower. *"Come, let us go down and confuse their language so they will not understand each other"* (Genesis 11:7, NIV).

It is especially important to listen to employee complaints. *"If I have despised the claim of my . . . [employees] when they filed a complaint against me, what then could I do when God arises? And when He calls me to account, what will I answer Him?"* (Job 31:13-15). A sensitive, listening ear is a tangible expression of care. When a complaint is legitimate, employers should take appropriate steps to solve the problem.

3. Hold employees accountable.

Employers are responsible for employees knowing what is expected on the job. Employers should regularly evaluate employee performance and communicate it to them. Employees who do not perform satisfactorily and are unable or unwilling to change may require dismissal.

4. Pay your employees a fair wage promptly.

The Bible warns employers to pay a fair wage. *"[The Lord will judge] those who oppress the wage earner in his wages"* (Malachi 3:5). It also commands them to pay wages promptly when due. *"You shall not oppress a hired [employee]. . . . Give him his wages on his day before the sun sets . . . so that he will not cry against you to the Lord and it become sin"* (Deuteronomy 24:14-15).

5. Pray for godly employees.

God may choose to bless an employer for having a godly employee. Scripture gives two examples of this. First, *"Laban said to [Jacob], 'If I have found favor in your eyes, please stay; . . . the Lord has blessed me because of you'"* (Genesis 30:27, NIV). Second, *"Joseph found favor in [Potiphar's] sight. . . . It came about that from the time he made [Joseph] overseer in his house and over all that he owned, the Lord blessed the Egyptian's house on account of Joseph; thus the Lord's blessing was upon all that he owned, in the house and in the field"* (Genesis 39:4-5).

This principle was my primary reason for employing Raymond, an especially godly construction worker. He was strong and did the work of two people, but far more important was his influence over the project. There was less profanity and pilferage, and he was an excellent model of hard work. This principle is not a command, but we believe wise employers will pray for God to bring "Raymonds" to their company.

HeyHoward@Crown.org

Q: *I've been using a spending plan and don't spend one cent on anything that is not an absolute need, but I'm still not able to make ends meet. What should I do?*

A: You're simply not earning enough money. You need to find a job for which you are well-suited that will produce more income. I'd start by taking an aptitude test to identify your best potential careers. Then pray and network like crazy to find the right job.

EMPLOYEE'S RESPONSIBILITIES

We can identify six major responsibilities of godly employees by examining the story of Daniel in the lion's den. In the sixth chapter of Daniel, Darius, the king of Babylon, appointed 120 people to administer the government, and three people—one of whom was Daniel—to supervise the administrators. Because of Daniel's outstanding service, King Darius decided to promote Daniel to govern the entire kingdom. Daniel's jealous peers looked for a way to disqualify him but could find no basis for accusation. Knowing Daniel's devotion to God, they asked King Darius to enact a law requiring everyone to worship only the king or die in the lion's den. Daniel refused to stop worshipping God, and Darius reluctantly threw him to the lions. When God rescued Daniel by sending an angel to shut the lions' mouths, the thankful king ordered all of his subjects to honor the God of Daniel. Daniel modeled the six characteristics of godly employees.

1. Honesty

Daniel 6:4 tells us that Daniel's fellow employees could find no dishonesty in him, and there was no "evidence of corruption" in his work. Daniel was an example of total honesty, the crucial character quality we studied in Week 5.

2. Faithfulness

We discover the second characteristic of godly employees in Daniel 6:4: *"He was faithful."* Godly employees strive for the goal of being faithful and excellent in work.

3. Prayerfulness

Godly employees are people of prayer. *"When Daniel knew that the document was signed [restricting worship to the king alone] . . . he continued kneeling on his knees three times a day, praying and giving thanks before his God, as he had been doing previously"* (Daniel 6:10). Daniel shouldered the responsibility of governing the most powerful country of his day. Few of us will ever face that kind of pressure or demands on our time. Yet he knew the importance of prayer. If you are not praying consistently, your work is suffering.

4. Loyalty—Honors Employer

"Daniel spoke to the king, 'O king, live forever!'" (Daniel 6:21). What a remarkable response from Daniel. The king had been tricked into sentencing Daniel to the lion's den. But Daniel's reaction was to honor his employer. Think how easy it would have been to disrespect the king and say something like, "You dummy! The God who sent His angel to shut the lions' mouths is now going to whack you!" Instead, he honored his employer.

Godly employees always honor their superiors. *"Servants [employees], be submissive to your masters [employers] with all respect, not only to those who are good and gentle, but also to those who are unreasonable"* (1 Peter 2:18). One way we honor employers is refusing to gossip behind their backs regardless of their weaknesses.

5. Honors Fellow Employees

People may damage your reputation or attempt to have you fired from your job to secure a promotion over you. Not only did they do that to Daniel, they even tried to murder him. Despite this, there is no evidence that he did anything but honor his fellow employees. *"Do not slander a servant [employee] to his master [employer], or he will curse you"* (Proverbs 30:10, NIV).

Godly employees avoid office politics and manipulation to secure a promotion. Your boss does not control your promotion; God does. You can be content in your job as you focus on being faithful, honoring superiors, and encouraging other employees. Having done this, you can rest, knowing that Christ will promote you if and when He chooses.

6. Verbalizes Faith

King Darius would never have known about God if Daniel had not communicated his faith at appropriate moments while at work. *"The king spoke and said to Daniel, 'Daniel, servant of the living God, has your God, whom you constantly serve, been able to deliver you from the lions?'"* (Daniel 6:20). Daniel's words and actions influenced King Darius, who observed his honesty, faithfulness, and hard work. Listen to the king's response: *"I issue a decree that in every part of my kingdom people must fear and reverence the God of Daniel. For He is the living God and He endures forever"* (Daniel 6:26, NIV).

Daniel influenced his employer, one of the most powerful people in the world, to believe in the only true God. You have that same opportunity in your God-given sphere of work. Let me say this another way. A job well done earns you the right to tell others with whom you work about the reality of Christ. Viewing your work from God's perspective turns dissatisfaction to contentment with a job well done; drudgery becomes excitement over the prospect of introducing others to the Savior.

OTHER WORK ISSUES

RETIREMENT

The dictionary defines retirement as "withdrawal from an occupation, retreat from an active life." Our culture promotes the goal of retirement and ceasing all labor to live a life filled with leisure. Is this a biblical goal?

Numbers 8:24-26—the only reference to retirement in Scripture—applied specifically to the Levites working in the tabernacle. While people are physically and mentally capable, there is no scriptural basis for retiring and becoming unproductive—the concept of putting an older but able person "out to pasture." Don't let age stop you from finishing the work God has called you to accomplish. He will provide you with the necessary strength. For example, Moses was 80 years old when he began his 40-year adventure of leading the children of Israel.

The Bible does imply, however, that the type or intensity of work may change as we grow older—shifting gears to a less demanding pace to become more of an "elder seated at the gate." During this season of life we can use the experience and wisdom gained over a lifetime. If we have sufficient income to meet our needs apart from our jobs, we may choose to leave work to invest more time in serving others as God directs.

AMBITION

Scripture does not condemn ambition. Paul was ambitious. *"We also have as our ambition . . . to be pleasing to Him"* (2 Corinthians 5:9). The Bible does, however, condemn selfish ambition. The Lord *"will render to each person according to his deeds . . . to those who are selfishly ambitious . . . wrath and indignation"* (Romans 2:6, 8). *"But if you have . . . selfish ambition in your heart, do not be arrogant and so lie against the truth. This wisdom is not that which comes down from above, but is earthly, natural, demonic. For where . . . selfish ambition exist, there is disorder and every evil thing"* (James 3:14-16). *"But you, are you seeking great things for yourself? Do not seek them"* (Jeremiah 45:5).

Remember, the Bible is not the enemy of ambition, only of the wrong type of ambition. Our ambition should be to please Christ, work hard and pursue excellence in our job to please Him.

YOUR CALLING

God has given each of us a specific calling or purpose. *"We are His workmanship, created in Christ Jesus for good works, which God prepared beforehand so that we would walk in them"* (Ephesians 2:10). Study this passage carefully. "We are His workmanship." The *Amplified® Bible* says, "We are His handiwork." God has given each of us special physical, emotional, and mental abilities. You may have heard the expression, "After the Lord made you, He threw away the mold." It's true! You are gifted uniquely. No one in all of history—past, present or future—is like you.

The passage continues, "created in Christ Jesus for good works, which God prepared beforehand so that we would walk in them." God created each of us for a particular task, endowing us with the abilities and desires to accomplish it. Your calling may be full-time Christian service or a secular job.

People often wonder whether God wants them to continue in their work after they commit their lives to Christ. Many feel they are not serving Him in a significant way if they remain at their jobs. Nothing could be further from the truth. The key is for each person to identify God's call for his or her life. Stanley Tam addresses this in his book, *God Owns My Business*: "Although I believe in the application of good principles in business, I place far more confidence in the conviction that I have a call from God. I am convinced that His purpose for me is in the business world. My business is my pulpit."

To those who earn a living through secular pursuits, it is a great comfort to know that the "call" of holy vocation carries over into all walks of life. The key is for us to identify God's call for our life, recognizing that God strategically places His children everywhere!

GOD STRATEGICALLY PLACES HIS CHILDREN EVERYWHERE!

PARTNERSHIPS

Scripture discourages business partnerships with those who do not know Christ. In 2 Corinthians 6:14-17 we read, *"Do not be bound together with unbelievers; for what partnership have righteousness and lawlessness, or what fellowship has light with darkness? . . . or what has a believer in common with an unbeliever? . . . 'Therefore, come out from their midst and be separate,' says the Lord."* Many have suffered financially for violating this principle.

In our opinion, we should be careful about entering into any partnership, even with another Christian. With my lifetime of contacts, I would consider only a few people as partners. These are people I know well. I have observed their commitment to the Lord. I know their strengths and weaknesses and have seen them handle money faithfully.

If, after prayerful consideration, you decide to form a partnership, first take the time to commit your understandings into writing. Develop this agreement with your future partner, and be sure to include a way to end the partnership. If you are not able to agree in writing, do not become partners. Remember, do not rush into a partnership!

PROCRASTINATION

A procrastinator is someone who, because of laziness or fear, has a habit of putting things off until later. This habit often develops into a serious character flaw.

The book of Ruth introduces Boaz, one of my favorite examples in the Bible of a non-procrastinator. Ruth's mother-in-law, Naomi, made this revealing comment about Ruth's future husband, Boaz: *"Wait, my daughter, until you know how the matter turns out; for the man will not rest until he has settled it today"* (Ruth 3:18). Boaz had a reputation for acting promptly.

Here are some practical suggestions to help overcome procrastination:

1. List the things you need to do each day.
2. Prayerfully review the list and prioritize it according to the tasks you need to accomplish first.
3. Finish the first task on your list before starting the second. Often that first task is the most difficult or the one you fear the most.
4. Ask God to give you courage, remembering Philippians 4:13, *"I can do all things through Him who strengthens me."*

WIVES WORKING OUTSIDE THE HOME

For many reasons, women work in jobs of all kinds. Married women work to provide additional income for their families, to express their creativity, or because they enjoy their jobs. Single women work to provide their needs.

In our opinion, unless family finances prohibit it, it is wise during the children's early formative years for the mother to be home while the children are home. Titus 2:4-5 reads, *"Encourage the young women to love their husbands, to love their children, to be sensible, pure, workers at home."* As the children mature, a mother will have increased freedom to pursue outside work.

Proverbs 31:10-27 reads, *"An excellent wife . . . does him [her husband] good and not evil all the days of her life. She looks for wool and flax and works with her hands. . . . She brings her food from afar. She rises also while it is still night and gives food to her household. . . . She considers a field and buys it; from her earnings she plants a vineyard. . . . She stretches out her hands to the distaff, and her hands grasp the spindle. She extends her hand to the poor. . . . She makes coverings for herself; her clothing is fine linen and purple. Her husband is known in the gates, when he sits among the elders of the land. She makes linen garments and sells them, and supplies belts to the tradesmen. . . . She looks well to the ways of her household, and does not eat the bread of idleness."*

Proverbs 31 paints a picture of the working wife living a balanced life with the thrust of her activity toward the home. Some women are gifted as homemakers; there is no more important task than raising godly children. Other women may have skills they desire to express in work outside the home, and some must work to earn income. Either way, it is a decision that the married couple should make together.

TWO-INCOME FAMILIES

If both the husband and wife work outside the home, it is worth examining how much income, after taxes and expenses, the second wage contributes. The "Example 1" column of the worksheet below makes the following assumptions: 40 hours a week at $9 per hour; giving 10 percent of the gross income; federal income tax of 25 percent (if a second income is added to the first, it may be taxed at an even higher rate); state income tax of 5 percent; Social Security tax of 7.5 percent; ten trips per week of five miles at a cost of 25 cents a mile; lunch, snacks, and coffee breaks of $15 per week; eating out more often and using convenience foods add $35 a week to the spending plan; $20 for extra clothing and cleaning; $5 more for grooming; extra child care of $45 a week. The "Example 2" column assumes earning $25 an hour; all other assumptions remain the same.

These assumptions are for illustration only and may not represent your situation. Complete the exercise below to determine your actual income after expenses.

Income and Spending for Second Wage Earner	Example 1	Example 2	My Situation
Gross yearly income	$18,720	$52,000	_____
Gross weekly income	$360	$1,000	_____
Expenses:			
Giving	$36	$100	_____
Federal income tax	$90	$250	_____
State income tax	$18	$50	_____
Social Security tax	$27	$75	_____
Transportation	$15	$15	_____
Lunch/snacks/breaks	$15	$15	_____
Restaurants/convenience food	$35	$35	_____
Extra clothing/cleaning	$20	$20	_____
Personal grooming	$5	$5	_____
Child care	$45	$45	_____
Total expenses	$306	$610	_____
Net additional family income	$54	$390	_____
Net income per hour	$1.35	$9.75	_____

Couples are often surprised to learn that the income earned by a second working spouse is not as much as they had expected. Some have actually produced more net income (after reducing work-related expenses) when they decided to work in some creative way while staying at home. Of course, the financial benefits are not the only factors to evaluate. Also consider the physical and emotional demands of working and how they affect a family.

"Steady plodding brings prosperity"
(Proverbs 21:5, TLB).

INVESTING

WEEK 8

Consistently save.

TO BE COMPLETED <u>PRIOR TO</u> WEEK 8 MEETING

Scripture to Memorize

"Steady plodding brings prosperity; hasty speculation brings poverty" (Proverbs 21:5, TLB).

Practical Application

Complete Saving and Investing, Insurance and Filing System, and review Destinations 4 and 5 on the *Crown Money Map.*™

Day One - Let's Review Work

Read the Work Notes on pages 92-100 and answer:

1. What in the notes proved especially helpful or challenging? How will this impact you?

2. Do you usually recognize you are working for the Lord? If not, what can you do to be more aware that you work for Him?

INVESTING

Day Two

Read Genesis 41:34-36; Proverbs 21:20; and Proverbs 30:24-25.

1. What do these passages say to you about savings?

   Genesis 41:34-36 –

   Proverbs 21:20 –

   Proverbs 30:24-25 –

2. If you are not yet saving, how do you propose to begin?

Read Luke 12:16-21, 34.

3. Why did the Lord call the rich man a fool?

4. According to this parable, why do you think it is scripturally permissible to save only when you are also giving?

Day Three

Read 1 Timothy 5:8.

1. What is a scripturally acceptable goal for saving?

Read 1 Timothy 6:9.

2. What is a scripturally unacceptable reason for saving?

Read 1 Timothy 6:10.

3. According to this verse, why is it wrong to want to get rich (refer to 1 Timothy 6:9)? Do you have the desire to get rich?

Read 1 Timothy 6:11.

4. What should you do if you have the desire to get rich?

Day Four

Read Proverbs 21:5; Proverbs 24:27; Proverbs 27:23-24; Ecclesiastes 3:1; and Ecclesiastes 11:2.

1. What investment principle(s) can you learn from each of these verses, and how will you apply each principle to your life?

    Proverbs 21:5 -

    Proverbs 24:27 -

    Proverbs 27:23-24 -

    Ecclesiastes 3:1 -

    Ecclesiastes 11:2 -

Day Five

Read Genesis 24:35-36; Proverbs 13:22; and 2 Corinthians 12:14.

1. Should parents attempt to leave a material inheritance to their children? Why or why not?

2. How are you going to implement this principle?

Read Proverbs 20:21 and Galatians 4:1-2.

3. What caution should a parent exercise?

    Proverbs 20:21 –

    Galatians 4:1-2 –

Day Six

Gambling is defined as: *playing games of chance for money and betting.* Some of today's most common forms of gambling are casino wagering, betting on sporting events, horse and dog races, and state-run lotteries.

1. What are some of the motivations that cause people to gamble?

2. Do these motives please the Lord? Why?

Read Proverbs 28:20 and Proverbs 28:22.

3. According to these passages, why do you think a godly person should not gamble (play lotteries, bet on sporting events)?

4. How does gambling contradict the scriptural principles of working diligently and being a faithful steward of the Lord's possessions?

Follow-up

☑ Please write your prayer requests in your prayer log before coming to the meeting.

☑ I will take the following action as a result of this week's study:

*TO BE READ **AFTER** COMPLETING YOUR WEEK 8 HOMEWORK*

The Bible contains very practical investing advice. But before we take a look at what it says about investing, we need to be aware of two important principles.

FINDING THE BALANCE: INVESTING AND GIVING

We need to balance our investing with generosity. Jesus told a parable of a farmer who harvested a bumper crop and said to himself, *"'I have no place to store my crops. . . . I will tear down my barns and build bigger ones, and there I will store all my grain and goods. . . .' But God said to him, 'You fool! . . . This is how it will be with anyone who stores up things for himself but is not rich toward God. . . . For where your treasure is, there your heart will be also'"* (Luke 12:16-21, 34).

The key word in this parable is *all*. Jesus called the farmer foolish because he saved everything. He didn't balance saving with giving. If we only pile up our investments, they will pull on our hearts like gravity. Our affection will be drawn away from God toward them because *"where your treasure is, there your heart will be also"* (Luke 12:34). However, if we give generously to God, we can invest and still love Him with all of our heart.

DANGER AHEAD

THE FIRST STEP IN INVESTING IS SAVING.

Let's face it—most people want to get rich. I'll never forget how surprised I was the first time I realized the Bible's caution against it: *"People who want to get rich fall into temptation and a trap and into many foolish and harmful desires that plunge men into ruin and destruction"* (1 Timothy 6:9). This verse says those who want to get rich give in to temptations and desires that ultimately lead to ruin. Wanting to get rich is incredibly dangerous, but why?

The next verse answers that question: *"For the love of money is a root of all kinds of evil. Some people, eager for money, have wandered away from the faith, and pierced themselves with many griefs"* (1 Timothy 6:10). When we want to get rich, we actually love money. That has consequences I witnessed firsthand. Mike, a close friend, became consumed by a desire to get rich. He finally abandoned his wife and four young sons and later denied Christ.

For much of my life I wanted to become rich—not just a little rich—filthy rich! So, dealing with this attitude has been difficult. Here is what I discovered: When I wanted to get rich, my motivations were pride, greed, or an urge to prepare for uncertain economic times. I loved money. However, when I desired to be a faithful steward and invest wisely the money God entrusted to me, my motive completely changed. I simply wanted to please Him. I loved God.

Understand, I am not saying it's wrong to become rich. Many heroes of the faith, such as Abraham and David, were rich. In fact, I rejoice when God enables a person who has been a faithful steward to prosper. Nothing is wrong with becoming wealthy if it is a by-product of being faithful.

OVERCOMING THE TEMPTATION

You can overcome the temptation to get rich by remembering to split and submit! Paul told Timothy to *"flee from [the desire to get rich], you man of God, and pursue righteousness, godliness, faith, love, perseverance and gentleness"* (1 Timothy 6:11). When you become aware of a desire to get rich, run from it! Analyze what triggers your desire. I discovered a habit of dreaming about wealth when I would take a long car trip. I broke the habit by listening to Christian radio to help me concentrate on the Lord.

The ultimate way of escape is submitting to God. We can do this confidently because Jesus overcame a huge temptation to become rich. After fasting 40 days, He was tempted three times by the devil. Here's the final temptation: *"He [the devil] led Him [Jesus] up and showed Him all the kingdoms of the world in a moment of time. And the devil said to Him, 'I will give You all this domain and its glory . . . if You worship before me'"* (Luke 4:5-7).

Jesus was offered all the kingdoms of the world. Because of His complete submission to the Father, He was empowered by the same Holy Spirit who lives in us to resist that temptation.

We believe that our heavenly Father does not usually allow His children to prosper when they are motivated to get rich. Wanting to get rich—loving money—closely parallels greed. And *"greed . . . amounts to idolatry"* (Colossians 3:5). It is for our sake that the Father protects us from loving anything that would draw us away from Him.

SAVING

The first step in investing is saving. Unfortunately, most people are not consistent savers.

Look at this graph. It's shocking! Americans saved an average of 10.8 percent of their income in 1984. By 2006, their rate of saving had fallen to a negative 1 percent, the lowest savings rate in the past 73 years!

The Bible, on the other hand, encourages us to save: *"The wise man saves for the future, but the foolish man spends whatever he gets"* (Proverbs 21:20, TLB). God commends the ant for saving. *"Four things on earth are small, yet they are extremely wise: Ants are creatures of little strength, yet they store up their food in*

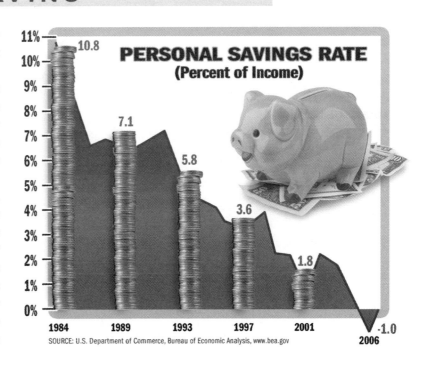

PERSONAL SAVINGS RATE
(Percent of Income)

11% — 10.8
10%
9%
8% — 7.1
7%
6% — 5.8
5%
4% — 3.6
3%
2% — 1.8
1%
0% — -1.0

1984   1989   1993   1997   2001   2006

SOURCE: U.S. Department of Commerce, Bureau of Economic Analysis, www.bea.gov

the summer" (Proverbs 30:24-25, NIV). We need to think like ants! Even though they are small, they save. You may not be in a position to save a lot right now, but begin the habit.

Joseph saved during "seven years of great abundance" (Genesis 41:29) in order to survive during "seven years of famine" (Genesis 41:30). That's what savings is all about: not spending today so that you will have something to spend in the future. Most people are poor savers because they don't see the value in practicing self-denial. Our culture screams that we deserve to get what we want, when we want it!

The most effective way to save is to make it automatic. When you receive income, the first check you write should be a gift to the Lord, and the second check should go to savings. An automatic payroll deduction is a great way to save. Some people save their tax refunds or bonuses. Remember this: if you immediately save, you'll save more.

The Bible doesn't teach an amount to be saved. We recommend saving 10 percent of your income. This may not be possible initially. But begin the habit of saving—even if it's only a dollar a month.

EMERGENCY SAVINGS

At Destination 1 on the *Crown Money Map*, you save $1,000 for emergencies—unexpected, unbudgeted expenses that whack us all. Then, increase emergency savings to three month's living expenses by Destination 3. Keep these savings in an account that is safe and easily accessible, such as, a money market account with check writing privileges.

UNDERSTANDING COMPOUND INTEREST

A wealthy man was asked if he had seen the seven wonders of the world. He responded, "No, but I do know the eighth wonder of the world—compounding." It's important to understand the three variables in compounding: the amount you save, the percentage rate you earn, and the length of time you save.

1. The Amount

The amount you save depends on your income and spending. We hope you will increase the amount available for saving as you learn God's way of handling money.

2. Rate of Return

The second variable is the rate you earn on an investment. The following table demonstrates how an investment of $1,000 a year grows at various rates.

Percent Earned	Year 5	Year 10	Year 20	Year 30	Year 40
6%	5,975	13,972	38,993	83,802	164,048
8%	6,336	15,645	49,423	122,346	279,781
10%	6,716	17,531	63,003	180,943	486,851
12%	7,115	19,655	80,699	270,293	859,142

As you can see, an increase in rate has a remarkable effect on the amount accumulated. A 2 percent increase almost doubles the total over 40 years. But since higher returns usually also carry higher risks, be careful not to shoot for unrealistic returns.

3. Time

Time is the third factor. Answer this: Who would accumulate more by age 65: Jennifer who started saving $1,000 a year at age 21, saved for eight years, and then completely stopped; or Matt who saved $1,000 a year for 37 years starting at age 29? Both earned 10 percent. Is it Jennifer who saved a total of $8,000 or Matt who saved $37,000? Check out the following chart. (It continues on the next page.)

| Age | JENNIFER | | MATT | |
	Contribution	Year-end Value	Contribution	Year-end Value
21	1,000	1,100	0	0
22	1,000	2,310	0	0
23	1,000	3,641	0	0
24	1,000	5,105	0	0
25	1,000	6,716	0	0
26	1,000	8,487	0	0
27	1,000	10,436	0	0
28	1,000	12,579	0	0
29	0	13,837	1,000	1,100
30	0	15,221	1,000	2,310
31	0	16,743	1,000	3,641
32	0	18,417	1,000	5,105
33	0	20,259	1,000	6,716
34	0	22,284	1,000	8,487
35	0	24,513	1,000	10,436
36	0	26,964	1,000	12,579
37	0	29,661	1,000	14,937
38	0	32,627	1,000	17,531
39	0	35,889	1,000	20,384
40	0	39,478	1,000	23,523
41	0	43,426	1,000	26,975
42	0	47,769	1,000	30,772
43	0	52,546	1,000	34,950
44	0	57,800	1,000	39,545
45	0	63,580	1,000	44,599
46	0	69,938	1,000	50,159
47	0	76,932	1,000	56,275
48	0	84,625	1,000	63,003
49	0	93,088	1,000	70,403
50	0	103,397	1,000	78,543
51	0	112,636	1,000	87,497
52	0	123,898	1,000	97,347
53	0	136,290	1,000	108,182
54	0	149,919	1,000	120,100

55	0	164,911	1,000	133,210
56	0	181,402	1,000	147,631
57	0	199,542	1,000	163,494
58	0	219,496	1,000	180,943
59	0	241,446	1,000	200,138
60	0	265,590	1,000	221,252
61	0	292,149	1,000	244,477
62	0	321,364	1,000	270,024
63	0	353,501	1,000	298,127
64	0	388,851	1,000	329,039
65	0	**$427,736**	1,000	**$363,043**
Total Investment	**$8,000**	**JENNIFER**	**$37,000**	**MATT**

Incredibly, Jennifer accumulated more because of the earlier start. So start saving now!

INVESTING

People place some of their savings in investments in the hope of receiving an income or growth in value. The purpose of this Crown Financial Ministries study is not to recommend any specific investments. No one is authorized to use affiliation with Crown to promote the sale of any investments or financial services. Our objective is to draw attention to the scriptural framework for savings and investing. Kingdom Advisors, led by Ron Blue and founded by Larry Burkett, is devoted to equipping Christian financial advisors to apply biblical wisdom to their advice and counsel. To learn more about the organization and its Qualified Kingdom Advisor™ designation, please visit KingdomAdvisors.org. Visit Crown's Web site for more detailed information on investing.

1. Be a steady plodder.

The fundamental principle for becoming a successful investor is to spend less than you earn and regularly invest the surplus. In other words, be a steady plodder. The Bible says, *"Steady plodding brings prosperity, hasty speculation brings poverty"* (Proverbs 21:5, TLB). The original words for "steady plodding" picture a person filling a large barrel one handful at a time. Little by little the barrel is filled. Nothing replaces consistent, month-after-month investing.

2. Avoid risky investments.

God warns us to avoid risky investments, yet each year thousands of people lose money in highly speculative investments and scams. The Bible says, *"There is another serious problem I have seen everywhere—savings are put into risky investments that turn sour, and soon there is nothing left to pass on to one's son. The man who speculates is soon back to where he began—with nothing"* (Ecclesiastes 5:13-15, TLB).

How many times have you heard of people losing their life's savings on a get-rich-quick scheme? Sadly, it seems that Christians are particularly vulnerable because they trust others who appear to live by their same values. The strategy for avoiding risky investments is to pray, seek wise counsel, and do your homework.

3. Diversify.

Money can be lost on any investment. Stocks, bonds, real estate, gold—you name it—can perform well or poorly. Each investment has its own advantages and disadvantages. Since the perfect investment doesn't exist, we need to diversify and not put all our eggs in one basket. *"Divide your portion to seven, or even to eight, for you do not know what misfortune may occur on the earth"* (Ecclesiastes 11:2).

4. Count the cost.

Every investment has costs: financial, time, effort, and sometimes even emotional stress. For example, a rental house will require time and effort to rent and maintain. If the tenant is irresponsible, you may have to try to collect rent from someone who doesn't want to pay—talk about emotions! Before you decide on any investment, consider all the costs.

WHAT GOD WANTS A SUCCESSFUL INVESTOR TO DO

God understands that when we increase our assets, they can become a potential barrier to an intimate relationship with Him. If you have a lot of resources, the Lord isn't disappointed or surprised; rather, He entrusted it to you for a purpose. In 1 Timothy 6:17-19, God gives us instructions to help those with resources to remain undistracted from loving Him.

1. Do not be conceited.

"Instruct those who are rich [successful investors] in this present world not to be conceited" (1 Timothy 6:17). Wealth tends to produce pride. For several years we drove two vehicles. The first was an old pickup truck that cost $100. It looked as if it cost $100! When I drove that truck to the bank drive-in window to cash a check, I was humble. I knew the cashier was going to carefully check my account to confirm that the driver of that beat-up truck had sufficient funds in his account. And when I received the money, I drove away with a song in my heart and praises on my lips.

Our other vehicle was a well-preserved, second-hand car that was expensive when it was new. When I drove that car to the bank, I appeared to be a different person. I was a person who deserved a certain amount of respect. I wasn't quite as patient when the cashier examined my account, and when I received the money I was not as grateful. Wealth often leads to pride.

2. Put no confidence in your assets.

"Instruct those who are rich in this present world not . . . to fix their hope on the uncertainty of riches, but on God, who richly supplies us with all things to enjoy" (1 Timothy 6:17).

The ability to accumulate assets without placing our confidence in them is a struggle. We tend to trust in the seen rather than in the invisible living God. It is easy to trust in money, because money can buy things. But we need to remind ourselves that possessions can be lost and that God alone can be fully trusted.

HeyHoward@Crown.org

Q: *I'm 55 years old. Is it too late for me to begin to save and invest?*

A: Absolutely not! No way! It's never too late to begin to apply God's financial principles. The key is simply to be faithful starting today.

Q: *I like investing in high-risk, high-return investments. Unfortunately, my wife does not feel comfortable with my approach. How can I convince her I'm right?*

A: Listen to her advice! God speaks most clearly to the husband through his wife.

3. Give generously.

"Instruct them to do good, to be rich in good works, to be generous and ready to share, storing up for themselves the treasure of a good foundation for the future, so that they may take hold of that which is life indeed" (1 Timothy 6:18-19). The Lord wants successful investors to be generous and tells them of two benefits: (1) eternal treasures that they will enjoy forever, and (2) the blessing of "taking hold of that which is life indeed." By exercising generosity, they can live the fulfilling life God intends for them now.

OTHER ISSUES

Gambling and Lotteries

Lotteries and gambling of all types are sweeping our country. Internet gambling is exploding. Each year one in four Americans gambles at a casino. The average church member gives $20 a year to international missions while the average person gambles $1,174 annually.

Sadly, more than 6 million Americans are addicted to gambling, with consequences that are heartbreaking for their loved ones. Although the Bible does not specifically prohibit gambling, its *get-rich-quick* motivation violates the steady plodding principle.

WE SHOULD NEVER PARTICIPATE IN GAMBLING OR LOTTERIES—EVEN FOR ENTERTAINMENT.

In my opinion, we should *never* participate in gambling or lotteries—even for entertainment. We should not expose ourselves to the risk of becoming compulsive gamblers, nor should we support an industry that enslaves so many.

Inheritance

Parents should try to leave an inheritance to their children. *"A good man leaves an inheritance to his children's children"* (Proverbs 13:22). But inheritances should not be dispensed until heirs have been trained to be wise stewards. *"An inheritance gained hurriedly at the beginning will not be blessed in the end"* (Proverbs 20:21). Consider sprinkling distributions over several years as heirs mature enough to handle the responsibility of money. Select trustworthy people to help supervise the finances of young heirs until they are capable stewards. *"As long as the heir is a child, he does not differ at all from a slave although he is owner of everything, but he is under guardians and managers until the date set by the father"* (Galatians 4:1-2).

Wills

It is important to prepare financially for your death. As Isaiah told Hezekiah, *"Thus says the Lord, 'Set your house in order, for you shall die'"* (2 Kings 20:1). One of the greatest gifts you can leave your loved ones for that emotional time is an organized estate and a properly prepared will or revocable living trust. If you don't have a current will or trust, make an appointment this week with an attorney to prepare one.

IT IS IMPORTANT TO PREPARE FINANCIALLY FOR YOUR DEATH.

THE ONE GUARANTEED INVESTMENT

I was 28 years old when I was exposed to the only guaranteed investment. I started attending a breakfast with several young businessmen. It wasn't long before I was impressed by their business savvy. But more than that, I was attracted to the quality of their lives. I didn't know what they had; but whatever it was, I wanted it.

These men spoke openly of their faith in God. I grew up going to church, but the religion I saw modeled for me meant nothing to me as an adult. I had concluded it was only a fairy tale until a friend described how I could enter into a personal relationship with Jesus Christ. He explained several truths from the Bible I had never understood before.

God loves you and wants you to know Him and experience a meaningful life.

God desires a close relationship with each of us. *"For God so loved the world, that He gave His only begotten Son, that whoever believes in Him shall not perish, but have eternal life"* (John 3:16). *"I [Jesus] came that they might have life, and have it abundantly"* (John 10:10).

When my son, Matt, was in the first grade, he wanted to win the 100-yard dash at his school's field day, but his classmate Bobby Dike was faster.

Field day finally arrived. They ran the 50-yard dash first, and Bobby beat Matt badly. I will never forget Matt coming up to me with tears in his eyes, "Dad, please pray for me in the 100-yard dash. I've just got to win." My heart sank as I nodded.

With the sound of the gun, Matt got off quickly. He pulled away from the rest of his classmates and won. I lost it, jumping and shouting with an exhilaration I had never before experienced. Then it occurred to me how much I loved my son. Although I love other people, I do not love them enough to give my son to die for them. But that is how much God the Father loved you. He gave His only Son, Jesus Christ, to die for you.

Unfortunately, we are separated from God.

God is holy—which simply means God is perfect, and He can't have a relationship with anyone who is not perfect. My friend asked if I had ever sinned—done anything that would disqualify me from perfection. "Many times," I admitted. He explained that every person has sinned, and the consequence of sin is separation from God. *"All have sinned and fall short of the glory of God"* (Romans 3:23). *"Your sins have cut you off from God"* (Isaiah 59:2, TLB).

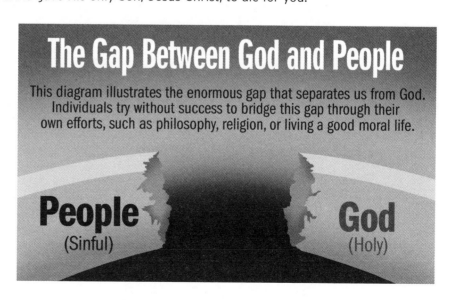

The Gap Between God and People

This diagram illustrates the enormous gap that separates us from God. Individuals try without success to bridge this gap through their own efforts, such as philosophy, religion, or living a good moral life.

People (Sinful)

God (Holy)

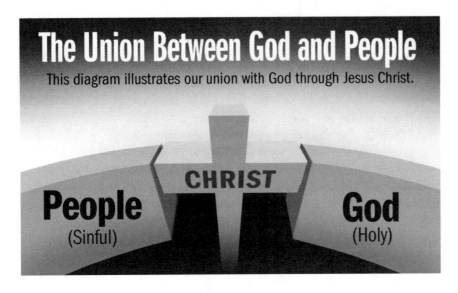

The Union Between God and People

This diagram illustrates our union with God through Jesus Christ.

People (Sinful)   CHRIST   **God** (Holy)

God's only provision to bridge this gap is Jesus Christ.

Jesus Christ died on the cross to pay the penalty for our sin, bridging the gap between God and us. Jesus said, *"I am the way, and the truth, and the life; no one comes to the Father but through Me"* (John 14:6). *"God demonstrates His own love towards us, in that while we were yet sinners, Christ died for us"* (Romans 5:8).

This diagram illustrates our union with God through Jesus Christ.

This relationship is a gift from God.

My friend explained that by faith I could receive the free gift of a relationship with God. The transaction appeared unfair. I had learned in business that a transaction happens only when both sides are convinced they are getting more than they are giving up. But now I was being offered a relationship with God, and it was free! *"It is by grace you have been saved, through faith—this is not from yourselves, it is the gift of God—not by works, so that no one can boast"* (Ephesians 2:8-9, NIV).

I had only to ask Jesus Christ to come into my life to be my Savior and Lord. So I did! As my friends will tell you, I am a very practical person—if something doesn't work, I stop doing it. I can tell you from more than 30 years of experience that a relationship with God works. And it is available to you through Jesus Christ. Nothing in life compares with knowing Christ personally. We can experience true peace, joy, and hope when we know him. It's the only way you can enjoy *true financial freedom*.

If you want to know God and are not certain whether you have this relationship, I encourage you to receive Jesus Christ right now. Pray a prayer similar to the one I prayed: "God, I need you. I'm sorry for my sin. I invite Jesus to come into my life as my Savior and Lord and to make me the person you want me to be. Thank you for forgiving my sins and giving me the gift of eternal life."

You might go all the way on your financial journey, but without a relationship with Christ, it won't have any lasting value. If you asked Christ into your life, you have made the most important decision anyone could ever make. I urge you to find a local church that teaches the Bible, one where you can begin to learn what it means to follow Jesus Christ.

"I have learned to be content in whatever circumstances I am. I know how to get along with humble means, and I also know how to live in prosperity. . . . I can do all things through Him who strengthens me"

(Philippians 4:11-13).

PERSPECTIVE

WEEK 9

Exercise wisdom when you spend.

Scripture to Memorize

"I have learned to be content in whatever circumstances I am. I know how to get along with humble means, and I also know how to live in prosperity. . . . I can do all things through Him who strengthens me" (Philippians 4:11-13).

Practical Application

Complete Organizing Your Estate, Draft a Will, and review Destination 6 on the *Crown Money Map*.™

Note: Think about your prayer request for the last meeting. It should be a "long-term" request the others can pray when they think of you.

Day One - Let's Review Investing

Read the Investing Notes on pages 108-116 and answer:

1. What in the notes proved especially helpful?

2. Describe the specific steps you intend to take to begin saving.

PERSPECTIVE

Day Two

Read Deuteronomy 30:15-16; Joshua 1:8; and Hebrews 11:36-40.

1. What do each of these passages communicate to you about financial prosperity for the believer?

Deuteronomy 30:15-16 –

Joshua 1:8 -

Hebrews 11:36-40 -

Reflect on the lives of Job (Job 1:8-21); Joseph (Genesis 37:23-28; 39:7-20); and Paul (2 Corinthians 11:23-27).

2. Did they ever experience periods of financial abundance and at other times a lack of financial prosperity?

3. Was their lack of financial prosperity a result of sin or lack of faith?

4. Should all Christians always prosper financially? Why?

Read Psalm 73:1-20.

5. What does this passage tell you about the prosperity of the wicked?

Day Three

Read Philippians 4:11-13 and 1 Timothy 6:6-8.

1. What do these passages say about contentment?

Philippians 4:11-13 -

1 Timothy 6:6-8 -

2. How does our culture discourage contentment?

3. How do you propose to practice contentment?

Day Four

Read Matthew 22:17-21 and Romans 13:1-7.

1. Does the Lord require us to pay taxes to the government? Why?

Read James 2:1-9.

2. What does Scripture say about partiality (showing favoritism)?

3. Are you guilty of partiality based on a person's financial, educational, or social status?

Read Romans 12:16 and Philippians 2:3.

4. How do you plan to overcome partiality?

Day Five

Read Acts 4:32-37 and 1 Thessalonians 4:11-12.

1. What do these passages communicate to you about lifestyle?

    Acts 4:32-37 -

    1 Thessalonians 4:11-12 -

2. How do the following factors influence your present spending and lifestyle?

    Comparing your lifestyle with that of friends and other people -

    Television, the Internet, magazines, catalogs, and other advertisements -

Your study of the Bible –

Your commitment to Christ and to things that are important to Him –

3. Do you sense that the Lord would have you change your spending or your standard of living? If so, in what way?

Day Six

Read Deuteronomy 6:6-7; Proverbs 22:6; and Ephesians 6:4.

1. According to these passages, who is responsible for teaching children how to handle money from a biblical perspective?

2. Stop and reflect for a few minutes: Describe how well you were prepared to manage money when you first left home as a young person.

3. Describe how you would train children to:

Create and maintain a spending plan –

Give –

Save –

Spend wisely –

Follow-up

☑ Please write your prayer requests in your prayer log before coming to the meeting.

☑ I will take the following action as a result of this week's study:

This chapter explores God's perspective on a variety of issues: lifestyle, prosperity, taxes, and teaching children about money.

LIFESTYLE

The Bible does not require one standard of living for everyone. God places His people in every level of society—rich and poor—just as He did in the pages of Scripture. To help us evaluate our standard of living, we examine several principles that should influence our lifestyle.

1. Learn to be content.

The apostle Paul wrote in 1 Timothy 6:8: *"If we have food and covering [clothes and shelter], with these we shall be content."* But our society operates on the assumptions that possessions equal happiness and more is always better. A modern ad would change Paul's message to read something like this, "If you can afford the finest food, wear the latest fashions, and live in a beautiful home, then you will be happy."

Six of the seven times the word "contentment" appears in the Bible, it involves money. Paul wrote, *"I have learned to be content in whatever circumstances I am. I know how to get along with humble means, and I also know how to live in prosperity; in any and every circumstance I have learned the secret of being filled and going hungry, both of having abundance and suffering need. I can do all things through Him who strengthens me"* (Philippians 4:11-13). Paul "learned" to be content. He was not born with this instinct, and neither are we; we must deliberately develop it.

The diagram below illustrates three elements to the secret of contentment.

KNOWING	+	DOING	+	TRUSTING	=	CONTENTMENT
what God requires of us in handling money and possessions		those requirements		God to provide exactly what He knows is best		

AM I SACRIFICING A CLOSE RELATIONSHIP WITH CHRIST IN THE PURSUIT OF WEALTH?

Merely knowing God's requirements is never enough to bring contentment; doing them is the key. We can trust our loving heavenly Father to provide exactly what He knows is best for us at any particular time—whether much or little. Biblical contentment has nothing to do with laziness or apathy. Because we serve the living and dynamic God, Christians should always seek to improve. Contentment does not exclude properly motivated ambition; instead, faithfully maximize the talents and possessions entrusted to you.

Biblical contentment is an inner peace that accepts what God has chosen for our present vocation and financial situation. *"Make sure that your character is free from the love of money, being content with what you have; for He Himself has said, 'I will never desert you, nor will I ever forsake you'"* (Hebrews 13:5).

2. Learn to avoid coveting.

Coveting means craving another's property, and Scripture prohibits it. The last of the Ten Commandments is, *"You shall not covet your neighbor's house; you shall not covet your neighbor's wife or his male servant or his female servant or his ox or his donkey or anything that belongs to your neighbor"* (Exodus 20:17). Note the broad application: "anything that belongs to your neighbor." In other words, do not covet anything that belongs to anyone!

Greed, which is similar to coveting, is strongly condemned. *"Do not let immorality or any impurity or greed even be named among you. . . . For this you know with certainty, that no immoral or impure person or covetous man, who is an idolater, has an inheritance in the kingdom of Christ and God"* (Ephesians 5:3, 5).

Greed and coveting have been called the silent sins. Rarely confronted, they are among the most common of sins. This is unfortunate, because they are a form of idolatry. When I began studying what the Bible teaches about money, I was overwhelmed by the extent of my own coveting. Ask God to show you if you are guilty of coveting something that is another's. If so, ask Him to change your heart.

3. Do not determine your lifestyle by comparing it to others.

Some use comparison to justify spending more than they should. Many have suffered financially because they insisted on "keeping up with the Joneses" even though they could not afford it. Someone once said, "You can never keep up with the Joneses. Just about the time you've caught them, they go deeper in debt to buy more stuff!"

4. Freely enjoy whatever God allows you to purchase.

Prayerfully submit spending decisions to God. Seeking His direction does not mean spending only for basic necessities.

During the Christmas season several years ago, my wife asked me to purchase a kitchen appliance that I considered extravagant. However, I promised to pray about it. As I prayed, He gave me peace about buying it, and we have enjoyed it thoroughly. *"Everything created by God is good, and nothing is to be rejected if it is received with gratitude"* (1 Timothy 4:4).

5. Make an effort to live more simply.

Every possession requires time, and often money, both to use and maintain. Too many or the wrong types of possessions can demand so much time or money that they harm our relationship with God and others. A quiet, simple life is the safest environment for us to be able to invest enough time to nurture relationships.

> *"Make it your ambition to lead a quiet life and attend to your own business and work with your hands, just as we commanded you, so that you will behave properly toward outsiders and not be in any need"* (1 Thessalonians 4:11-12).

Do not become unduly encumbered with the cares of this life. *"Suffer hardship with me, as a good soldier of Christ Jesus. No soldier in active service entangles himself in the affairs of everyday life, so that he may please the one who enlisted him as a soldier"* (2 Timothy 2:3-4).

6. Success is meaningless apart from serving Jesus Christ.

King Solomon, the author of Ecclesiastes, had an annual income of more than $35 million. He lived in a palace that took 13 years to build. He owned 40,000 stalls of horses. His household's daily menu required 100 sheep and 30 oxen.

Obviously, Solomon was in a position to know whether money could bring true happiness. He concluded, *"Vanity of vanities . . . all is vanity!"* (Ecclesiastes 12:8). Nothing, even extraordinary success, can replace the value of our relationship with God. Ask yourself this question: Am I sacrificing a close relationship with Christ in the pursuit of wealth? *"What does it profit a man to gain the whole world, and forfeit his soul?"* (Mark 8:36).

7. Do not be conformed to this world.

Romans 12:2 says, *"Do not be conformed to this world."* The *Amplified® Bible* says it this way: *"Do not be conformed to this world (this age), fashioned after and adapted to its external, superficial customs."* We live in one of the most affluent cultures the world has ever known. Powerfully effective advertisements constantly tempt us to spend money by stressing the importance of image over function. For example, a car ad rarely focuses on its merits as reliable transportation; instead, it projects an image of status or sex appeal.

No matter what the product—clothing, deodorants, credit cards, or anything else—the message is clear: The happy, beautiful, wrinkle-free life can be ours if we are willing to buy it. Unfortunately, this has influenced all of us to some extent. Author George Fooshee states it well, "People buy things they do not need with money they do not have to impress people they do not even like."

This graph depicts how the artificial, media-driven lifestyle influences our lives. The bottom curve represents our income—what we can afford to buy. The next curve illustrates what we actually spend. We make up the difference between our income and spending by the use of debt, which creates stress. The top of the graph demonstrates what advertisers tell us to buy—the expensive lifestyle that falsely claims to satisfy our deepest needs. When we want to live this unaffordable dream, we suffer discontentment.

From time to time we all get hooked on something we think we must buy. Once hooked, it is easy to rationalize any purchase. Remember to seek the Lord's guidance and godly counsel when making spending decisions.

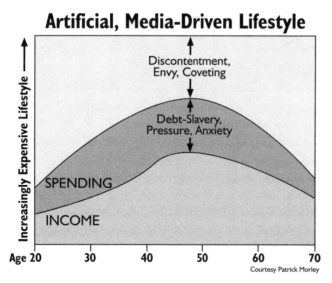

Artificial, Media-Driven Lifestyle

Increasingly Expensive Lifestyle →

Discontentment, Envy, Coveting

Debt-Slavery, Pressure, Anxiety

SPENDING

INCOME

Age 20   30   40   50   60   70

Courtesy Patrick Morley

POVERTY, PROSPERITY, OR STEWARDSHIP?

Many Christians embrace one of two extreme financial philosophies. The first elevates poverty in the belief that a wealthy person cannot have a close relationship with Christ. However, not only does the Bible not say this, a number of godly people in it were among the wealthiest individuals of their day.

In the Old Testament, God extended the reward of abundance for obedience and the threat of poverty as a consequence of disobedience. *"I have set before you today life and prosperity, and death and adversity; in that I command you today to love the Lord your God, to walk in His ways and to keep His commandments . . . that the Lord your God may bless you"* (Deuteronomy 30:15-16).

Psalm 35:27 says, *"The Lord . . . delights in the prosperity of His servant."* We may pray for prosperity when our relationship with God is healthy and we have a proper perspective on possessions. *"Beloved, I pray that in all respects you may prosper and be in good health, just as your soul prospers"* (3 John 2).

The other extreme, also an error, treats prosperity as the constant entitlement of all Christians who truly have faith. Study the life of Joseph, a faithful person who experienced both prosperity and poverty. Born into a prosperous family, his jealous brothers sold him into slavery. While a slave, Joseph's master promoted him to be head of his household. In that capacity, he was tempted but made the right choice not to commit adultery with his master's wife. That choice cost him many years in jail, but in God's timing, he was ultimately elevated to prime minister of Egypt.

The guideline for prosperity is found in Joshua 1:8, *"This book of the law shall not depart from your mouth, but you shall meditate on it day and night, so that you may be careful to do according to all that is written in it; for then you will make your way prosperous, and then you will have success."*

This passage offers two requirements for prosperity. Meditate on the Scriptures and do everything they command. When you do this, you place yourself in a position for God to entrust you with resources. There is no guarantee, however, that you will always prosper financially. Consider these four reasons of why the godly may not prosper.

1. Violating Scriptural Principles

Look again at Joshua 1:8. There is the requirement to do all that is written in the Bible. A person may be giving generously but acting dishonestly. A person may be honest but not fulfilling work responsibilities. A person may be a faithful employee but head-over-heels in debt. A person may be completely out of debt but not giving. One of the benefits of this study is that we explore what the entire Bible teaches about money. Those who do not understand all the requirements often neglect areas of responsibility unknowingly and suffer financially.

2. Building Godly Character

Many of the Bible's godly people lived righteously and yet lost their possessions. After slaying Goliath and becoming a national hero, David had to flee for his life from a tormented King Saul. Job lost his children and possessions in the space of a few moments and was described as a *"blameless and upright man, fearing God and turning away from evil"* (Job 1:8). Paul learned the secret of contentment while suffering in prison even though he was righteous.

God sometimes molds our character by allowing us to experience difficult circumstances. An example of how the Lord develops character in a people before prospering them is found in Deuteronomy 8:16-18: *"In the wilderness He fed you manna which your fathers did not know, that He might humble you and that He might test you, to do good for you in the end. Otherwise, you may say in your heart, 'My power and the strength of my hand made me this wealth.' But you shall remember the Lord your God, for it is He who is giving you power to make wealth."* Our Father knows us better than we know ourselves. In His infinite wisdom, He knows exactly how much He can entrust to us at any time without it harming us.

3. Our Dependence and His Discipline

A father was carrying his two-year-old daughter as he waded in a lake. While they were close to shore, the child was unconcerned because of the apparent safety of the beach even though the water was deep enough to drown her. She didn't understand her dependence upon her father. The farther they moved away from shore, the tighter she held to her father. Like the child, we are always completely dependent upon God to provide for us even when we don't recognize it because we are close to the shore of apparent financial security. But when our possessions are limited, it is easier to recognize our need and cling to Him.

And since even the godly sometimes stray, Hebrews 12:6, 10 tells us *"The Lord disciplines those he loves . . . for our good, so that we may share in his holiness"* (NIV). If we harbor unconfessed sin or a wrong attitude toward money, out of the Lord's great love for us He may discipline us by allowing financial difficulties to encourage us to forsake our sin.

4. The Mystery of God's Sovereignty

Hebrews 11 records "Faith's Hall of Fame." Verses 1-35 list people who triumphed miraculously by the exercise of their faith in God. Then in verse 36, the writer directs our attention to godly people who gained God's approval and yet experienced poverty. God ultimately chooses how much to entrust to each person, sometimes for reasons beyond our comprehension.

	POVERTY	STEWARDSHIP	PROSPERITY
Possessions are	Evil	A responsibility	A right
I work to	Meet only basic needs	Serve Christ	Become rich
Godly people are	Poor	Faithful	Wealthy
Ungodly people are	Wealthy	Unfaithful	Poor
I give	Because I must	Because I love God	To get
My spending is	Without gratitude to God	Prayerful and responsible	Carefree and consumptive

LET'S SUMMARIZE: The Scriptures teach neither the necessity of poverty nor uninterrupted prosperity. What the Bible teaches is the responsibility to be a faithful steward. Please review this chart contrasting the three perspectives.

It is important to understand that God evaluates true riches based on His spiritual value system, which is stated most clearly in Revelation. The godly poor are rich in

God's sight. *"I [the Lord] know your tribulation and your poverty (but you are rich)"* (Revelation 2:9). Those who are wealthy without enjoying a close relationship with Christ are actually poor. *"You say, 'I am rich, and have become wealthy, and have need of nothing,' and you do not know that you are wretched and miserable and poor and blind and naked"* (Revelation 3:17). True prosperity extends far beyond material possessions. We can gauge it by how well we know Jesus Christ and how closely we follow Him.

DANGERS OF PROSPERITY

Remember that God loves you deeply and wants to enjoy a close relationship with you. Because of His love, the Lord reveals dangers associated with money that can damage our relationship with Him and others. First, wealth tends to separate people. Abram and Lot were relatives. Their prosperity ultimately caused them to move away from each other. *"Abram was very rich in livestock, in silver and in gold. . . . [Lot] also had flocks and herds and tents. And the land could not sustain them while dwelling together, for their possessions were so great that they were not able to remain together"* (Genesis 13:2, 5-7). You probably know friends or family who have allowed conflicts over money to damage their relationships.

Second, it is easy for those who are prosperous to turn from God. *"When I [the Lord] bring them into the land . . . and they have eaten and are satisfied and become prosperous, then they will turn to other gods and serve them, and spurn Me"* (Deuteronomy 31:20). After people become prosperous, they often take the Lord for granted, thinking they no longer need Him. Paul warned Timothy, *"Instruct those who are rich in this present world not . . . to fix their hope on the uncertainty of riches, but on God"* (1 Timothy 6:17).

Third, it is difficult for the rich to come to know Jesus Christ as their Savior. *"Jesus said to His disciples, 'Truly I say to you, it is hard for a rich man to enter the kingdom of heaven'"* (Matthew 19:23). Again, this is because the rich generally feel less of a need for God.

Fourth, riches can destroy a spiritually fruitful life. *"The one on whom seed was sown among the thorns, this is the man who hears the word, and the worry of the world and the deceitfulness of wealth choke the word, and it becomes unfruitful"* (Matthew 13:22). Riches are deceitful because they are tangible and can blind us from the reality of the unseen Lord. They seem capable of doing things that only Christ can really do.

WHY DO THE WICKED PROSPER?

This is a question God's people have asked for centuries. The prophet Jeremiah inquired of God: *"You are always righteous, O Lord. . . . Yet I would speak with you about your justice: Why does the way of the wicked prosper?"* (Jeremiah 12:1, NIV).

The Psalmist asked the same question when it seemed that godliness did not "pay off." Then the Lord revealed the wicked person's end—sudden eternal punishment:

"Surely God is good to . . . those who are pure in heart. But as for me. . . I envied the arrogant when I saw the prosperity of the wicked. . . . When I tried to understand all this, it was oppressive to me till I entered the sanctuary of God; then I understood their final destiny. Surely you place them on slippery

HeyHoward@Crown.org

Q: *How often should I review my will?*

A: Review it every three years—even sooner if you or your family experience significant changes or there is a change to the tax law.

ground; you cast them down to ruin. How suddenly are they destroyed, completely swept away by terrors!" (Psalm 73:1-3, 16-19, NIV).

The Bible tells us not to worry about or envy the wicked who prosper, because life on earth is short. "Do not fret because of evil men or be envious of those who do wrong; for like the grass they will soon wither, like green plants they will soon die" (Psalm 37: 1-2, NIV). We are to maintain God's perspective and His eternal value system.

LITIGATION

Thousands of lawsuits are filed each day in our country. Unfortunately, many of these pit Christian against Christian. Suing seems to be a national pastime. A woman accused a man of kicking her at a nightclub and sued him for $200,000 compensation for the injury and lost time on the dance floor!

Many factors contribute to this flood of lawsuits, including an avalanche of new laws and, most disturbing, a growing tendency for people to be less and less forgiving. The court system uses an adversarial process, which frequently creates animosities between the parties involved. Instead of trying to heal, the system provides a legal solution but leaves the problems of unforgiveness and anger untouched.

The Bible stresses the goal of reconciliation. "If you are presenting your offering at the altar, and there remember that your brother has something against you, leave your offering there before the altar and go; first be reconciled to your brother" (Matthew 5:23-24).

Scripture states that when Christians are at odds with one another, they should not settle their disputes through the courts. "Does any one of you, when he has a case against his neighbor, dare to go to law before the unrighteous and not before the saints? Or do you not know that the saints will judge the world? If the world is judged by you, are you not competent to constitute the smallest law courts? Do you not know that we shall judge angels? How much more matters of this life? So if you have law courts dealing with matters of this life, do you appoint them as judges who are of no account in the church? I say this to your shame. Is it so, that there is not among you one wise man who will be able to decide between his brethren, but brother goes to law with brother, and that before unbelievers? Actually, then, it is already a defeat for you, that you have lawsuits with one another. Why not rather be wronged? Why not rather be defrauded?" (1 Corinthians 6:1-7).

Instead of initiating a lawsuit, a three-step procedure for Christians to resolve their differences is set forth in Matthew 18:15-17: "If your brother sins, go and show him his fault in private; if he listens to you, you have won your brother. But if he does not listen to you, take one or two more with you, so that by the mouth of two or three witnesses every fact may be confirmed. And if he refuses to listen to them, tell it to the church; and if he refuses to listen even to the church, let him be to you as a Gentile and a tax-collector."

1. **Go in private.** The person who believes he or she has been wronged needs to confront the other party in private with specific claims. If the dispute remains unresolved,

2. **Go with one or two others.** The person who feels wronged should return with witnesses who can confirm facts or help resolve the dispute. If this is unsuccessful,
3. **Go before the church.** The third step is mediation or arbitration before church leadership or perhaps a conciliation service sponsored by a church or ministry.

The greatest benefit of following this procedure is not merely reaching a fair settlement of the dispute but practicing forgiveness and demonstrating love.

TAXES

What does God say about paying taxes? Someone asked Jesus that very question: *"Is it lawful for us to pay taxes to Caesar, or not? . . . [Jesus] said to them, 'Show Me a denarius [Roman coin]. Whose likeness and inscription does it have?' They said, 'Caesar's.' And He said to them, 'Then give to Caesar the things that are Caesar's'"* (Luke 20:22-25). This is an example of the contrast between the practices of our society and the teaching of Scripture. Avoid paying taxes people rationalize; after all, the government waste so much money.

But the Bible tells us to pay our taxes: *"Every person is to be in subjection to the governing authorities. For there is no authority except from God, and those which exist are established by God. . . . Because of this you also pay taxes, for rulers are servants of God, devoting themselves to this very thing. Render to all what is due them: tax to whom tax is due"* (Romans 13:1, 6-7). It is permissible to reduce taxes by using legal tax deductions, but we should be careful not to make unwise decisions simply to avoid paying taxes.

PARTIALITY

Study this passage carefully. *"Do not hold your faith in our glorious Lord Jesus Christ with an attitude of personal favoritism. For if a man comes into your assembly with a gold ring and dressed in fine clothes, and there also comes in a poor man in dirty clothes, and you pay special attention to the one who is wearing the fine clothes . . . have you not made distinctions among yourselves, and become judges with evil motives? . . . If, however, you are fulfilling the royal law according to the Scripture, 'You shall love your neighbor as yourself,' you are doing well. But if you show partiality, you are committing sin and are convicted by the law as transgressors"* (James 2:1-9).

ONE PRACTICAL WAY TO OVERCOME PARTIALITY IS TO CONCENTRATE ON THE ABILITIES OF EACH PERSON.

I have struggled with the sin of partiality and its unintentional influence on my actions. Once, when I hung up the phone, my wife said, "I know you were not talking to Ken; it must have been Ryan. You like Ken better, and it shows in your voice."

Partiality can be based on more than just a person's wealth. Other causes may be education, social position, or spiritual status. James 2:9 could not be more blunt: *"If you show partiality, you are committing sin and are convicted by the law as transgressors."* How do we break the habit of partiality? Romans 12:10 tells us, *"Be devoted to one another in brotherly love; give preference to one another in honor."* And Philippians 2:3 reads, *"With humility of mind regard one another as more important than yourselves."*

We need to ask God to help us develop the habit of elevating each person to be more important than ourselves. One practical way to overcome partiality is to concentrate on the abilities of each person. Everyone can do some things better than I can. This realization helps me appreciate all people.

TEACHING CHILDREN

In 1904, the country of Wales experienced a remarkable revival. Thousands of people were introduced to Christ, and it produced dramatic results. Bars closed due to lack of customers. Policemen exchanged their weapons for white gloves because crime disappeared. Wales was so evangelistically minded that it sent missionaries all over the world.

One of those missionaries traveled to the streets of Argentina, where he led a young boy to Christ. The boy's name was Luis Palau, now known as the "Billy Graham of Latin America." Many years later, Palau visited Wales to express his gratitude for being led to Christ. What he discovered was astonishing: less than one-half of one percent of the Welsh attended church. Divorce was at an all-time high and crime was increasing. The impact of Christianity had all but disappeared.

In response, Palau produced a film titled *God Has No Grandchildren*. The thrust of the film is that each generation is responsible for passing on the faith to the next.

Each generation is responsible for passing on the truths of Scripture, including God's financial principles, to its children. Proverbs 22:6 says, *"Train up a child in the way he should go, even when he is old he will not depart from it."*

Answer this question: When you left home, how well prepared were you to make financial decisions? Parents and teachers spend years preparing young people for occupations but generally less than a few hours teaching children the value and use of the money they will earn during their careers.

Parents should be MVP parents. MVP is an acronym that describes the three methods to teach children God's way of handling money: Modeling, Verbal communication, and Practical opportunities. All three are needed to train your children. Let's look at each.

MODELING

Since children soak up parental attitudes toward money like a sponge soaks up water, parents must model handling money wisely. Paul recognized the importance of modeling when he said, *"Be imitators of me, just as I also am of Christ"* (1 Corinthians 11:1).

Luke 6:40 is a challenging passage. It reads, *"Everyone, after he has been fully trained, will be like his teacher."* Another way of saying this is that we can teach what we believe, but we only reproduce who we are. We must be good models.

VERBAL COMMUNICATION

The Lord charged the Israelites, *"These words, which I am commanding you today, shall be on your heart. You shall teach them diligently to your sons and shall talk of them when you sit in your house and when you walk by the way and when you lie down and when you rise up"* (Deuteronomy 6:6-7). We must verbally instruct children in the ways of the Lord, but children need more than verbal instruction; they also need a good example.

PRACTICAL EXPERIENCE

Children then need to be given opportunities to apply what they have heard and seen. There are learning experiences that benefit the child in the area of money management and money making.

LEARNING EXPERIENCES IN MANAGING MONEY

Learning to handle money should be part of a child's education. This is something parents must direct themselves and not delegate to teachers because spending occurs outside the classroom. Consider five areas in which this is possible.

1. Income

As soon as children are ready for school, they should begin to receive incomes to manage. Decide whether children should earn the income or receive it as an allowance.

The amount will vary with the child's age, ability to earn, and the financial circumstances of the family. The amount is not as important as the responsibility of handling money. At first it is a new experience, and children will make many mistakes. Do not hesitate to let the "law of natural consequences" run its course. You will be tempted to help when they immediately spend it all on an unwise purchase. But do not bail them out! Mistakes will be their best teacher.

Parents should establish boundaries and offer advice on how to spend, but children must have freedom of choice within those boundaries. The first few dimes and quarters will make a lasting impression.

Every Saturday I used to bicycle to the store with my son, Matthew, to buy him a pack of gum. Despite my advice, he would consume the entire pack that day. When he started to earn money, we decided that he should buy his gum. I will never forget the pained expression on his face as he came out of the store with his first purchase. "This gum cost me all my money!" he moaned. But he rationed it carefully and it lasted the entire week. Parents should slowly increase the income as children grow in ability and demonstrate wise spending patterns.

2. Spending Plan

When children begin receiving an income, teach them how to create and maintain a spending plan. Use a simple system, a three-compartment bank with each compartment labeled separately: GIVE, SAVE, and SPEND. Children distribute a portion of their income into each compartment, creating a simple plan that uses visual control. Even a six-year-old can understand this method, because when the spending compartment is empty, he can't buy anything more!

As children mature, they should participate in the family spending plan to help them understand the limitations of the family income. When they become teenagers, they should begin a written spending plan. Encourage them to use a budgeting software program. Help them to become wise consumers by teaching shopping skills, the ability to distinguish needs from wants, and the importance of waiting on God to provide. Warn them about the powerful influence of advertising and the danger of impulse spending.

3. Saving and Investing

Establish the habit of saving as soon as children receive an income. Begin by helping them open a savings account in their name. As they mature, expose them to various types of investments: stocks, bonds, real estate, etc. Teach them the benefits of compounding. If they grasp this concept and become faithful savers, they will enjoy financial stability as adults. Demonstrate this by saving for something that will directly benefit them. Using a graph they can fill in helps them visually chart the progress of saving.

Children should have both short-term and long-term saving goals. The younger the child, the more important short-term goals are. To four-year-olds, a week seems like a lifetime to save for a purchase. They will not understand saving for their future education but will get excited about saving for a small toy.

4. Debt

One way to teach children to avoid debt is to show them how difficult it is to get out of debt. A father loaned his son and daughter money to buy bicycles. He drew up a repayment schedule that included the interest charged. After the children completed the long process of paying off the loan, the family celebrated with a "mortgage burning" ceremony. The children appreciated those bikes more than any of their other possessions and vowed to avoid debt in the future.

5. Giving

Early childhood is the best time to establish the habit of giving. It is helpful for children to give a portion of their gifts to a tangible need they can see. For example, when their gift helps to build the church under construction or buy food for a needy family they know, they can understand its impact.

Richard Halverson, former U. S. Senate chaplain, gave his son, Chris, this heritage as a child. Chris gave money to support Kim, an orphan who had lost his sight during the Korean War, and thought of Kim as an adopted brother. One Christmas, Chris bought Kim a harmonica. Kim cherished this gift from Chris and learned to play it well. Today, Kim is an evangelist with a gospel presentation that includes playing the harmonica.

Teens benefit enormously by serving at a local homeless shelter or taking a mission trip to a country where there is deep poverty. This exposure can initiate a lifetime of giving to the poor. We also recommend a family time each week for dedicating that week's gifts to the Lord.

LEARNING EXPERIENCES IN MAKING MONEY

Parents are also responsible for training children to develop proper work habits. Children who learn to enjoy work and are faithful at it will become productive and valuable in the job market where good employees are difficult to find. There are four areas to consider in this training.

1. Learning Routine Responsibilities

The best way for young children to learn to work is to establish daily household chores for each member of the family.

2. Exposing Your Children to Your Work

Many children do not know how their fathers or mothers earn income. An important way to teach the value of work is to expose children to the parents' means of making a living.

One word of advice: Because children are not usually with their parents at work, parents' work habits around the home will be a major influence. If a parent works hard away from home but complains about washing the dishes, what is being communicated to the children about work? Examine your work activities at home to ensure that you are properly influencing them.

3. Working for Others

Baby-sitting, bagging groceries, or waiting on tables is an education. When children enter into an employee-employer relationship to earn extra money, they can learn the value of work and how to deal with others. Children who work with a good attitude are more satisfied and grow up with greater respect for the value of money and the effort required to earn it.

4. Career Direct—YES!®

The *Career Direct—Youth Exploration Survey®* points students ages 13 to 16 toward a fulfilling future career. It covers four areas: personality, vocational interests, abilities, and priorities. Designed to be fun, informative, and interactive, it is biblically based and can be used by individuals or groups. To order, contact Crown.

PRAYER

One of the more valuable lessons you can teach children is to seek the Lord's guidance and provision through prayer. God wants to demonstrate that He is actively involved in our lives. One way He does this is by answering our prayers. We often rob ourselves of this opportunity by buying things or charging purchases without praying for God to supply them.

One couple decided to ask their son to pray for some shirts he needed. After several months, a friend in the clothing business called to ask if their son needed shirts because he had excess inventory in his size. They responded, "Absolutely!" and the friend brought 10 shirts to their home. That evening as their son began to pray for shirts, the father said, "You don't need to pray for those anymore; God has answered that prayer." One by one they brought out the shirts. By shirt 10, their son thought God must be in the shirt business.

SINGLE PARENTS AND GRANDPARENTS

Single Parents

Single parents are increasingly common, and if you are one, we appreciate the added demands you face. Be encouraged—God defends the cause of single-parent families: *"He executes justice for the orphan and the widow, and shows His love . . . by giving him food and clothing"* (Deuteronomy 10:18). And He sustains the fatherless: *"The Lord . . . supports the fatherless and the widow"* (Psalm 146:9). Some of the most faithful children I have ever met were raised by single parents.

Grandparents

If you are a grandparent, you have a special opportunity to influence your grandchildren because of the unique role you can play. Unfortunately, many parents and grandparents have not agreed on how to train the next generation, leading to bruised relationships and ineffective training. Because grandparents can be very effective in complementing the objectives of parents, we recommend that they meet together to design a strategy for training their next generation to handle money.

STRATEGY FOR INDEPENDENCE

Finally, it is wise to establish a strategy for independence. Lyle and Marge Nelsen, parents of four mature and responsible children, had their children manage all of their own finances (with the exception of food and shelter) by their senior year in high school. That way they were available to advise the children as they learned to make spending decisions.

As the people of Wales discovered, God has no grandchildren. Passing our faith in Christ to the next generation can be compared to a relay race. Any track coach will tell you that relay races can be won or lost in the passing of the baton from one runner to another. Runners rarely drop the baton once it is firmly in their grasp. If it is going to be dropped, it is in the exchange between the runners. Adults have the responsibility to pass the baton of practical biblical truths to the younger generation. This happens through training that sometimes shows little progress, but we urge you to be consistent and persistent! May our generation leave our children the blessed legacy of financial faithfulness.

Startling Statistics

• *Seventy percent of Americans die without a current will.*

"What does it profit a man to gain the whole world, and forfeit his soul?"
(Mark 8:36).

ETERNITY

WEEK 10

All will give an account.

Scripture to Memorize

"What does it profit a man to gain the whole world, and forfeit his soul?" (Mark 8:36).

Practical Application

Complete My Life Goals and review Destination 7 and Long-Term Goals on the *Crown Money Map.*™

Also, complete the Involvement and Suggestions Survey in the Life Group section of Crown.org.

Day One - Let's Review Perspective

Read the Perspective Notes on pages 124-136 and answer:

1. What was the most helpful concept you learned from the notes?

2. Do you sense the Lord would have you alter your lifestyle in any way? If so, in what way?

ETERNITY

Day Two

Read Psalm 39:4-6 and Psalm 103:13-16.

1. What do these passages say to you about the length of life on earth?

Read Psalm 90:10, 12.

2. Why did Moses ask God to teach us to number our days?

3. Estimate the number of days you have left on earth. How does this impact your thinking?

4. Based on your number of days, what actions will you take?

Day Three

Read 1 Chronicles 29:15; Philippians 3:20; and 1 Peter 2:11.

1. What do these passages say about your identity on earth and in heaven?

   1 Chronicles 29:15 -

   Philippians 3:20 -

   1 Peter 2:11 -

Read 2 Peter 3:10-13.

2. What will happen to the earth?

3. How should this impact the way you invest your time and spend money?

Day Four

Read Ecclesiastes 12:13-14 and 2 Corinthians 5:9-10.

1. What will happen to each of us in the future?

    Ecclesiastes 12:13-14 –

    2 Corinthians 5:9-10 –

Read 1 Corinthians 3:11-15.

2. How would you describe the works (give some examples) that will be burned at this final judgment?

3. Give some examples of works that will be rewarded.

4. What are you doing that will survive this final judgment?

Day Five

Read 2 Corinthians 4:18.

1. What does this verse say to you?

2. As you reflect on eternity, answer this question thoughtfully: What three things do I want to accomplish during the rest of my life?

3. What can I do during my lifetime that would contribute most significantly to the cause of Christ?

4. In light of these answers, what actions or changes do I need to make?

Day Six

Read the Eternity Notes on pages 144-151 and answer:

1. What was the most important concept you learned from reading the notes?

2. Please complete the Involvement and Suggestions Survey in the Life Group section of Crown.org.

3. Describe what has been the most beneficial part of the *Biblical Financial Study* for you:

Follow-up

☑ Please write your prayer requests in your prayer log before coming to the meeting.

☑ I will take the following action as a result of this week's study:

On Monday, October 25, 1999, the news reported an unfolding story. Air Force jets following a Lear jet from Orlando, Florida, were unable to communicate with its pilots. I learned later that two very close friends, Robert Fraley and Van Ardan, were on that Lear as it carried them and golfer Payne Stewart to their deaths.

One of the most critical principles for us to understand when handling money is the reality of eternity. Robert and Van were men in their mid-forties who lived with an eternal perspective. Robert had framed these words in his workout area, "Take care of your body as though you will live forever; take care of your soul as if you will die tomorrow."

Because God loves us, He reveals in the Bible that there is a heaven and a hell, that there is a coming judgment, and that He will grant eternal rewards. The Lord wants the very best for us. Therefore, He wants to motivate us to invest our lives and finances in such a way that we can enjoy an intimate relationship with Him now and receive the greatest possible rewards and responsibilities in heaven.

Our failure to view our present lives through the lens of eternity is one of the biggest hindrances to seeing our lives and our finances in their true light. Yet Scripture states that the reality of our eternal future should determine the character of our present lives and the use of our money and possessions.

People who do not know the Lord look at life as a brief interval that begins at birth and ends at death. Looking to the future, they see no further than their own life span. With no eternal perspective, they think, if this life is all there is, why deny myself any pleasure or possession?

Those who know Christ have an entirely different perspective. We know life is short; it is the preface—not the book; it is the preliminary—not the main event. This testing period will determine much of our experience in heaven.

Financial planners try to convince people to look down the road instead of simply focusing on today. "Don't think in terms of this year," they will tell you. "Think and plan for 30 years from now." The wise person does indeed think ahead, but far more than 30 years—30 million years ahead. Someone once said, "He who provides for this life but takes no care for eternity is wise for a moment but a fool forever." Jesus said it this way, *"What does it profit a man to gain the whole world, and forfeit his soul?"* (Mark 8:36).

EARTHLY GOODS WILL NOT LAST FOREVER—THEY ARE DESTINED FOR ANNIHILATION.

THE LONG AND SHORT OF IT

The Bible frequently reminds us that life on earth is brief: *"[God] is mindful that we are but dust"* (Psalm 103:14). Our earthly bodies are called "tents" (2 Peter 1:13, NIV), temporary dwelling places of our eternal souls. David recognized this and sought to gain God's perspective on the brevity of life. He asked of God, *"Show me, O Lord, my life's end and the number of my days; let me know how fleeting is my life. . . . Each man's life is but a breath. Man is a mere phantom . . . he heaps up wealth, not knowing who will get it"* (Psalm 39:4-6, NIV).

When a good friend discovered she had only a short time to live, she told me of her radical change in perspective. "The most striking thing that's happened," she said, "is that I find myself almost totally uninterested in accumulating more things. Things used to matter to me, but now I find my thoughts are centered on Christ, my friends, and other people."

Moses realized that true wisdom flowed out of understanding that our lives are short. So he asked the Lord to help him number the days he had on earth. *"As for the days of our life, they contain seventy years, or if due to strength, eighty years . . . for soon it is gone and we fly away. . . . So teach us to number our days, that we may present to You a heart of wisdom"* (Psalm 90:10, 12).

I encourage you to number the days you estimate that you have left on earth. If I live as long as my father, I have about 8,000 days left. This has helped me become aware that I need to invest my life and resources in eternally important matters.

When I served in the Navy, I was very interested in the town in which I was stationed. However, as soon as I received orders discharging me in two months, I became what was called a "short-timer." My interest completely shifted from the town I was leaving to the town that would become my new home. In a similar way, when we realize that we are really "short-timers" on earth and will soon be going to our real home, our focus will shift to what is important in heaven. Author Matthew Henry said, "It ought to be the business of every day to prepare for our last day."

"IT OUGHT TO BE THE BUSINESS OF EVERY DAY TO PREPARE FOR OUR LAST DAY."
- MATTHEW HENRY

Eternity Is Long

Eternity, on the other hand, never ends. It is forever. Imagine a cable running through the room where you are now. To your right, the cable runs millions of light years all the way to the end of the universe; to your left, it runs to the other end of the universe. Now imagine that the cable to your left represents eternity past, and the cable to your right, eternity future. Place a small mark on the cable in front of you; the mark represents your brief life on earth.

Because most people do not have an eternal perspective, they live as if the mark were all there is. They make mark choices, living in mark houses, driving mark cars, wearing mark clothes, and raising mark children. Devotional writer A. W. Tozer referred to eternity as "the long tomorrow." This is the backdrop against which all the questions of life and the handling of our resources must be answered.

ALIENS AND PILGRIMS

Scripture tells us several things about our identity and role on earth. First, *"Our citizenship is in heaven"* (Philippians 3:20), not earth. Second, *"We are ambassadors for Christ"* (2 Corinthians 5:20), representing Him on earth. Imagine yourself as an ambassador working in a country that is generally hostile to your own. Naturally, you want to learn about this new place, see the sights, and become familiar with the people and culture. But suppose you eventually become so assimilated into this foreign country that you begin to regard it as your true home. Your allegiance wavers, and you gradually compromise your position as an ambassador, becoming increasingly ineffective in representing the best interests of your own country.

We must never become too much at home in this world or we will become ineffective in serving the cause of the kingdom we are here to represent. We are aliens, strangers, and pilgrims on earth. Peter wrote, *"Live your lives as strangers here in reverent fear"* (1 Peter 1:17, NIV). Later he added, *"I urge you, as aliens and strangers in the world, to abstain from sinful desires"* (1 Peter 2:11, NIV). Another Bible translation uses the words "strangers and pilgrims" (KJV).

Pilgrims are unattached. They are travelers—not settlers—aware that the excessive accumulation of things can distract. Material things are valuable to pilgrims but only as they facilitate their mission. Things can entrench us in the present world, acting as chains around our legs that keep us from moving in response to God. When our eyes are too focused on the visible, they will be drawn away from the invisible. *"So we fix our eyes not on what is seen, but on what is unseen. For what is seen is temporary, but what is unseen is eternal"* (2 Corinthians 4:18, NIV).

Pilgrims of faith look to the next world. They see earthly possessions for what they are: useful for kingdom purposes but far too flimsy to bear the weight of trust. Thomas à Kempis, author of *The Imitation of Christ*, said it this way, "Let temporal things serve your use, but the eternal be the object of your desire." Two principles concerning possessions help us gain a proper perspective of them.

1. We Leave It All Behind.

After wealthy John D. Rockefeller died, his accountant was asked how much he left. The accountant responded, "He left it all." Job said it this way, *"Naked I came from my mother's womb, and naked I shall return there"* (Job 1:21). Paul wrote, *"We have brought nothing into the world, so we cannot take anything out of it either"* (1 Timothy 6:7).

The psalmist observed, *"Do not be afraid when a man becomes rich . . . for when he dies he will carry nothing away; his glory will not descend after him. Though while he lives he congratulates himself—and though men praise you when you do well for yourself—he shall go to the generation of his fathers"* (Psalm 49:16-20).

2. Everything Will Be Destroyed.

Earthly goods will not last forever—they are destined for annihilation. *"The day of the Lord will come like a thief. The heavens will disappear with a roar; the elements will be destroyed by fire, and the earth and everything in it will be laid bare. Since everything will be destroyed in this way, what kind of people ought you to be? You ought to live holy and godly lives"* (2 Peter 3:10-11, NIV). Understanding the temporary nature of possessions should influence us as we consider spending decisions.

JUDGMENT

It is uncomfortable to think about judgment. But because our Lord loves us so deeply, He wants us to realize what will happen in the future. Therefore, God revealed to us that we all will be judged according to our deeds: *"He has fixed a day in which He will judge the world in righteousness"* (Acts 17:31). All of us should live each day with this awareness: *"They will have to give an account to Him who is ready to judge the living and the dead"* (1 Peter 4:5, NIV).

God will judge us with total knowledge: *"Nothing in all creation is hidden from God's sight. Everything is uncovered and laid bare before the eyes of Him to whom we must give account"* (Hebrews 4:13, NIV). Because His knowledge is total, his judgment is comprehensive: *"Men will have to give account on the day of judgment for every careless word they have spoken"* (Matthew 12:36, NIV). His judgment extends to what is hidden from people. *"God will bring every deed into judgment, including every hidden thing, whether it is good or evil"* (Ecclesiastes 12:14, NIV). He will even *"disclose the motives of men's hearts"* (1 Corinthians 4:5).

The Bible teaches that all those who do not know Christ will be judged and sent to an indescribably dreadful place. *"I saw a great white throne and Him who was seated on it . . . and I saw the dead, great and small, standing before the throne. . . . Each person was judged according to what he had done. . . . If anyone's name was not found written in the book of life, he was thrown into the lake of fire"* (Revelation 20:11-15, NIV).

Judgment of Believers

After they die, those who know Christ will spend eternity with God in heaven, an incredibly wonderful place. But what we seldom consider is that the entry point to heaven is a judgment.

Scripture teaches that all believers in Christ will give an account of their lives to the Lord. *"We shall all stand before the judgment seat of God. . . . So then each of us will give an account of himself to God"* (Romans 14:10, 12). The result of this will be the gain or loss of eternal rewards. In 1 Corinthians 3:13-15 (NIV) we read, *"His work will be shown for what it is, because the [Judgment] Day will bring it to light. . . . If what he has built survives, he will receive his reward. If it is burned up, he will suffer loss."* Our works are what we have done with our time, influence, talents, and resources. God's Word does not treat this judgment as just a meaningless formality before we get on to the real business of heaven. Rather, Scripture presents it as a monumental event in which things of eternal significance are brought to light.

MOTIVATION AND REWARDS

Why should I follow God's guidance on money and possessions when it is so much fun to do whatever I please with my resources? I'm a Christian. I know I'm going to heaven anyway. Why not have the best of both worlds—this one and the next? Though few of us would be honest enough to use such language, these questions reflect a common attitude.

The prospect of eternal rewards for our obedience is a neglected key to unlocking our motivation. Paul was motivated by the prospect of eternal rewards. He wrote, *"I have fought the good fight, I have finished the course, I have kept the faith; in the future there is laid up for me the crown of righteousness, which the Lord, the righteous Judge, will award to me on that day"* (2 Timothy 4:7-8). God appeals not only to our compassion but also to our eternal self-interest. *"Love your enemies, and do good, and lend, expecting nothing in return; and your reward will be great"* (Luke 6:35).

Our heavenly Father uses three things to motivate us to obey Him: the love of God, the fear of God, and the rewards of God. These are the same things that motivate my children to obey me. Sometimes their love for me is sufficient motivation, but other times it isn't. In a healthy sense, they also fear me. They know I will discipline them for

HeyHoward@Crown.org

Q: *Why is it important to write down my financial goals?*

A: Writing down your goals is powerful because it helps you clarify your thinking, monitor your progress, and make midcourse corrections.

wrongdoing. They also know I will reward them with my words of approval and sometimes in tangible ways for doing right.

Unequal Rewards in Heaven

It is not as simple as saying, "I'll be in heaven and that's all that matters." On the contrary, Paul spoke about the loss of reward as a terrible loss. The receiving of rewards from Christ is a phenomenal gain. Not all Christians will have the same rewards in heaven.

John Wesley said, "I value all things only by the price they shall gain in eternity." God's kingdom was the reference point for him. He lived as he did, not because he did not treasure things but because he treasured the right things. We often miss something in missionary martyr Jim Elliot's famous words, "He is no fool who gives what he cannot keep to gain what he cannot lose." We focus on Elliot's willingness to sacrifice, and so we should; however, we often overlook his motivation for gain. What separated him from many Christians was not that he didn't want treasure but that he wanted real treasure. Remember God loves you deeply. Because He wants the best for you throughout eternity, God has revealed that today's financial sacrifices and service for Him will pay off forever.

IMPACTING ETERNITY TODAY

Our daily choices determine what will happen in the future. What we do in this life is of eternal importance. We only live on this earth once. *"It is appointed for men to die once and after this comes judgment"* (Hebrews 9:27). There is no such thing as reincarnation. Once our life on earth is over, we will never have another chance to move the hand of God through prayer, to share Christ with one who does not know the Savior, to give money to further God's kingdom, or to share with the needy.

Those who dabble in photography understand the effect of the "fixer." In developing a photograph, the negatives are immersed in several different solutions. The developing solution parallels this life. As long as the photograph is in the developing solution, it is subject to change. But when it is dropped in the fixer or "stop bath," it is permanently fixed, and the photograph is done. So it will be when we enter eternity: The life each of us lives on earth will be fixed as is, never to be altered or revised.

Alfred Nobel was a Swedish chemist who made a fortune by inventing dynamite and explosives for weapons. When Nobel's brother died, a newspaper accidentally printed Alfred's obituary instead. He was described as a man who became rich by enabling people to kill each other with powerful weapons. Shaken from this assessment, Nobel resolved to use his fortune to reward accomplishments that benefit humanity. We now know those rewards as the Nobel Peace Prize. Let us put ourselves in Nobel's place. Let us read our own obituary, not as written by people but as it would be written from heaven's point of view. Then let us use the rest of our lives to edit that obituary into what we really want it to be.

I loved playing Little League Baseball as a young boy. We played on a huge diamond with towering fences in the outfield. Years later, shortly after my father died, I spent the day walking around my old hometown reflecting on his life. When I visited the baseball field, I was shocked. It was so small! I could actually step over the outfield fences. While standing there, a thought struck me: Many of those things that seem so large and important to us today shrink to insignificance in just a few years.

When I am face to face with Christ and look back on my life, I want to see that the things in which I invested my time, creativity, influence, and money are big things to Him. I do not want to squander my life on things that will not matter throughout eternity.

During Moses' time, Pharaoh was the most powerful person on earth. Pharaoh's daughter adopted Moses as an infant, giving him the opportunity to enjoy the wealth and prestige of a member of the royal family. Hebrews 11:24-26 tells us what Moses later chose and why. *"By faith Moses, when he had grown up, refused to be called the son of Pharaoh's daughter, choosing rather to endure ill-treatment with the people of God than to enjoy the passing pleasures of sin, considering the reproach of Christ greater riches than the treasures of Egypt; for he was looking to the reward."* Because Moses was looking forward to the only rewards that would last, he chose to become a Hebrew slave and was used by God in a remarkable way.

What are the choices facing you now? How does an eternal perspective influence your decisions? Martin Luther said his calendar consisted of only two days: "today" and "that Day." May we invest all that we are and have today in light of that day.

LET'S REVIEW

At the beginning of this study, we asked why the Bible says so much about money and possessions—in more than 2,350 verses. We offered four reasons:

1. How we handle money impacts our fellowship with God.
2. Money is the primary competitor with Christ for the lordship of our life.
3. Money molds our character.
4. The Lord wants us to have a road map for handling money so that we can become financially faithful in very practical ways.

Review this diagram of the wheel, identifying the eight areas of our responsibilities, each with its primary thrust.

Faithfulness is a journey.

Applying the financial principles of the Bible is a journey that takes time. It's easy to become discouraged when your finances aren't completely under control by the end of this study. It takes the average person at least a year to apply most of these principles, and even longer if you have made financial mistakes. Many graduates decide to lead this study because they know the leaders learn more than anyone else. As they help their life group members, the leaders make progress on their own journey to true financial freedom.

Faithfulness in small matters is foundational.

Some people become frustrated by the inability to solve their financial problems quickly. Remember, simply be faithful with what you have—whether it is little or much. Some abandon the goal of becoming debt free or increasing their saving or giving because the task looks impossible. And perhaps it is—without God's help. Your job is to make a genuine effort, no matter how small it may appear, and then leave the results to God. I love what God said to the prophet Zechariah, *"For who has despised the day of small things?"* (Zechariah 4:10). Don't be discouraged. Be persistent. Be faithful in even the smallest matters. We have repeatedly seen God bless those who tried to be faithful.

NOW IS THE TIME!

We are not economists, but we recognize the probability that our country will experience financially difficult times in the future. We don't know when this will occur or exactly what it will look like, but we believe God has graciously given us a window of time to conform to His Word in the area of money. We plead with you to seize this opportunity! Become diligent in your efforts to get out of debt, give generously, stick to a spending plan, and work as unto the Lord. In short, become a faithful steward.

Now that you know the biblical framework for managing money, you have half of the solution. The other half is that you must apply what you have learned. Jesus said, *"Everyone who hears these words of Mine and acts on them, may be compared to a wise man who built his house upon the rock. And the rain fell, and the floods came, and the winds blew and slammed against that house; and yet it did not fall, for it had been founded on the rock. Everyone who hears these words of Mine and does not act on them, will be like a foolish man who built his house on the sand. The rain fell, and the floods came, and the winds blew and slammed against that house; and it fell, and great was its fall"* (Matthew 7:24-27).

Economic rain, floods, and winds will someday come against this country's financial house. If you have acted and built your house upon the rock-solid principles of Scripture, your house will not fall. One of the best ways to demonstrate your love for your family and friends is to get your financial house in order and encourage others to do the same.

If you have a desire to help others learn God's way of handling money, we encourage you to serve in one of four places illustrated in the baseball diamond. First, you may serve individuals as a life group leader or Money Map Coach. These are the heroes of Crown Financial Ministries, because it is in the life group or one-on-one where lives change most. Second base represents the opportunity to impact your entire church by serving as a church coordinator or on the church team. Maybe you have a desire to influence your community; third base is for those who serve on a city team. Larger cities require a full-time director and a team of volunteers. Finally, home plate is for those who have a "missionary spirit" and wish to help introduce Crown to other cities and even other countries.

Please tell your leader if you wish to become a leader or co-leader or to serve on your church team. If you want to serve your entire city or beyond, contact Crown Financial Ministries at Crown.org.

We appreciate the effort you have invested in this study. And we pray this has given you a greater appreciation for the Bible, helped you develop close friendships, and above all, nurtured your love for Jesus Christ. May God richly bless you on your journey to true financial freedom.

"When we've been there ten thousand years,
Bright shining as the sun,
We've no less days to sing God's praise
Than when we'd first begun."

−John P. Rees, Stanza 5, *Amazing Grace*

MY NOTES

"Pray for one another. . . . The effective prayer of a righteous man can accomplish much"

(James 5:16).

PRAYER LOGS

ALWAYS PRAY

Be faithful in prayer.

"Pray for one another" (James 5:16).

Name _____   Spouse _____

Home phone _____   Children (ages) _____

Business phone _____   _____

Mobile phone _____   _____

E-mail _____   _____

Home address _____   _____

_____   _____

Week	Prayer Request(s)	Answers to Prayer
1		
2		
3		
4		
5		
6		
7		
8		
9		
10	*My long-term prayer request:*	

"Pray for one another" (James 5:16).

Name _____   Spouse _____

Home phone _____   Children (ages) _____

Business phone _____   _____

Mobile phone _____   _____

E-mail _____   _____

Home address _____   _____

_____   _____

Week	Prayer Request(s)	Answers to Prayer
1		
2		
3		
4		
5		
6		
7		
8		
9		
10	*My long-term prayer request:*	

"Pray for one another" (James 5:16).

Name _____   Spouse _____

Home phone _____   Children (ages) _____

Business phone _____   _____

Mobile phone _____   _____

E-mail _____   _____

Home address _____   _____

_____   _____

Week	Prayer Request(s)	Answers to Prayer
1		
2		
3		
4		
5		
6		
7		
8		
9		
10	*My long-term prayer request:*	

"Pray for one another" (James 5:16).

Name _____   Spouse _____

Home phone _____   Children (ages) _____

Business phone _____   _____

Mobile phone _____   _____

E-mail _____   _____

Home address _____   _____

_____   _____

Week	Prayer Request(s)	Answers to Prayer
1		
2		
3		
4		
5		
6		
7		
8		
9		
10	*My long-term prayer request:*	

"Pray for one another" (James 5:16).

Name _____   Spouse _____

Home phone _____   Children (ages) _____

Business phone _____   _____

Mobile phone _____   _____

E-mail _____   _____

Home address _____   _____

_____   _____

Week	Prayer Request(s)	Answers to Prayer
1		
2		
3		
4		
5		
6		
7		
8		
9		
10	*My long-term prayer request:*	

"Pray for one another" (James 5:16).

Name _____   Spouse _____

Home phone _____   Children (ages) _____

Business phone _____   _____

Mobile phone _____   _____

E-mail _____   _____

Home address _____   _____

_____   _____

Week	Prayer Request(s)	Answers to Prayer
1		
2		
3		
4		
5		
6		
7		
8		
9		
10	*My long-term prayer request:*	

"Pray for one another" (James 5:16).

Name _____   Spouse _____

Home phone _____   Children (ages) _____

Business phone _____   _____

Mobile phone _____   _____

E-mail _____   _____

Home address _____   _____

_____   _____

Week	Prayer Request(s)	Answers to Prayer
1		
2		
3		
4		
5		
6		
7		
8		
9		
10	*My long-term prayer request:*	

"Pray for one another" (James 5:16).

Name _____   Spouse _____

Home phone _____   Children (ages) _____

Business phone _____   _____

Mobile phone _____   _____

E-mail _____   _____

Home address _____   _____

_____   _____

Week	Prayer Request(s)	Answers to Prayer
1		
2		
3		
4		
5		
6		
7		
8		
9		
10	*My long-term prayer request:*	

"Pray for one another" (James 5:16).

Name _____   Spouse _____

Home phone _____   Children (ages) _____

Business phone _____   _____

Mobile phone _____   _____

E-mail _____   _____

Home address _____   _____

_____   _____

Week	Prayer Request(s)	Answers to Prayer
1		
2		
3		
4		
5		
6		
7		
8		
9		
10	*My long-term prayer request:*	

"Pray for one another" (James 5:16).

Name _____ Spouse _____

Home phone _____ Children (ages) _____

Business phone _____ _____

Mobile phone _____ _____

E-mail _____ _____

Home address _____ _____

_____ _____

Week	Prayer Request(s)	Answers to Prayer
1		
2		
3		
4		
5		
6		
7		
8		
9		
10	*My long-term prayer request:*	

"Pray for one another" (James 5:16).

Name _____   Spouse _____

Home phone _____   Children (ages) _____

Business phone _____   _____

Mobile phone _____   _____

E-mail _____   _____

Home address _____   _____

_____   _____

Week	Prayer Request(s)	Answers to Prayer
1		
2		
3		
4		
5		
6		
7		
8		
9		
10	*My long-term prayer request:*	